COMPREHENSIVE RESEARCH
AND STUDY GUIDE

BLOOM'S
MAJOR
SHORT
STORY
WRITERS

Mark
Twain

EDITED AND WITH AN
INTRODUCTION BY HAROLD BLOOM

BLOOM'S MAJOR DRAMATISTS

Anton Chekhov

Henrik Ibsen

Arthur Miller

Eugene O'Neill

Shakespeare's Comedies

Shakespeare's Histories

Shakespeare's Romances

Shakespeare's Tragedies

George Bernard Shaw

Tennessee Williams

BLOOM'S MAJOR NOVELISTS

Jane Austen

The Brontës

Willa Cather

Charles Dickens

William Faulkner

F. Scott Fitzgerald

Nathaniel Hawthorne

Ernest Hemingway

Toni Morrison

John Steinbeck

Mark Twain

Alice Walker

BLOOM'S MAJOR SHORT STORY WRITERS

William Faulkner

F. Scott Fitzgerald

Ernest Hemingway

O. Henry

James Joyce

Herman Melville

Flannery O'Connor

Edgar Allan Poe

J. D. Salinger

John Steinbeck

Mark Twain

Eudora Welty

BLOOM'S MAJOR WORLD POETS

Geoffrey Chaucer

Emily Dickinson

John Donne

T. S. Eliot

Robert Frost

Langston Hughes

John Milton

Edgar Allan Poe

Shakespeare's Poems & Sonnets

Alfred, Lord Tennyson

Walt Whitman

William Wordsworth

BLOOM'S NOTES

The Adventures of Huckleberry Finn

Aeneid

The Age of Innocence

Animal Farm

The Autobiography of Malcolm X

The Awakening

Beloved

Beowulf

Billy Budd, Benito Cereno, & Bartleby the Scrivener

Brave New World

The Catcher in the Rye

Crime and Punishment

The Crucible

Death of a Salesman

A Farewell to Arms

Frankenstein

The Grapes of Wrath

Great Expectations

The Great Gatsby

Gulliver's Travels

Hamlet

Heart of Darkness & The Secret Sharer

Henry IV, Part One

I Know Why the Caged Bird Sings

Iliad

Inferno

Invisible Man

Jane Eyre

Julius Caesar

King Lear

Lord of the Flies

Macbeth

A Midsummer Night's Dream

Moby-Dick

Native Son

Nineteen Eighty-Four

Odyssey

Oedipus Plays

Of Mice and Men

The Old Man and the Sea

Othello

Paradise Lost

A Portrait of the Artist as a Young Man

The Portrait of a Lady

Pride and Prejudice

The Red Badge of Courage

Romeo and Juliet

The Scarlet Letter

Silas Marner

The Sound and the Fury

The Sun Also Rises

A Tale of Two Cities

Tess of the D'Urbervilles

Their Eyes Were Watching God

To Kill a Mockingbird

Uncle Tom's Cabin

Wuthering Heights

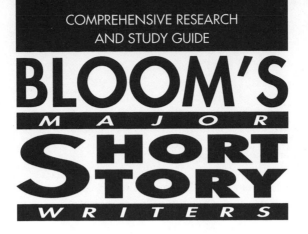

COMPREHENSIVE RESEARCH
AND STUDY GUIDE

BLOOM'S
MAJOR
SHORT
STORY
WRITERS

Mark
Twain

EDITED AND WITH AN INTRODUCTION BY HAROLD BLOOM

3 5 7 9 8 6 4 2

Library of Congress Cataloging-in-Publication Data

Mark Twain / edited and with an introduction by Harold Bloom.
p.   cm. — (Bloom's major short story writers)
Includes biographical references and index.
ISBN 0-7910-5124-2 (hc)
1. Twain, Mark, 1835–1910—Criticism and interpretation—Handbooks,
manuals, etc.   2. Twain, Mark, 1835–1910—Examinations—Study guides.
3. Short story—Examinations—Study guides.   4. Short story—
Handbooks, manuals, etc.
I. Bloom, Harold.   II. Series.
PS1338.M27   1999
818'.409—dc21
98–54082
CIP

Chelsea House Publishers
1974 Sproul Road, Suite 400
Broomall, PA 19008-0914

Contributing Editor: Elizabeth Beaudin

Contents

User's Guide

This volume is designed to present biographical, critical, and bibliographical information on the author's best-known or most important short stories. Following Harold Bloom's editor's note and introduction is a detailed biography of the author, discussing major life events and important literary accomplishments. A plot summary of each short story follows, tracing significant themes, patterns, and motifs in the work, and an annotated list of characters supplies brief information on the main characters in each story.

A selection of critical extracts, derived from previously published material from leading critics, analyzes aspects of each short story. The extracts consist of statements from the author, if available, early reviews of the work, and later evaluations up to the present. A bibliography of the author's writings (including a complete list of all books written, cowritten, edited, and translated), a list of additional books and articles on the author and the work, and an index of themes and ideas in the author's writings conclude the volume.

~

Harold Bloom is Sterling Professor of the Humanities at Yale University and Henry W. and Albert A. Berg Professor of English at the New York University Graduate School. He is the author of over 20 books and the editor of more than 30 anthologies of literary criticism.

Professor Bloom's works include *Shelley's Mythmaking* (1959), *The Visionary Company* (1961), *Blake's Apocalypse* (1963), *Yeats* (1970), *A Map of Misreading* (1975), *Kabbalah and Criticism* (1975), and *Agon: Toward a Theory of Revisionism* (1982). *The Anxiety of Influence* (1973) sets forth Professor Bloom's provocative theory of the literary relationships between the great writers and their predecessors. His most recent books include *The American Religion* (1992), *The Western Canon* (1994), *Omens of Millennium: The Gnosis of Angels, Dreams, and Resurrection* (1996), and *Shakespeare: The Invention of the Human* (1998).

Professor Bloom earned his Ph.D. from Yale University in 1955 and has served on the Yale faculty since then. He is a 1985 MacArthur Foundation Award recipient and served as the Charles Eliot Norton Professor of Poetry at Harvard University in 1987–88. He is currently the editor of other Chelsea House series in literary criticism, including BLOOM'S NOTES, BLOOM'S MAJOR POETS, MAJOR LITERARY CHARACTERS, MODERN CRITICAL VIEWS, MODERN CRITICAL INTERPRETATIONS, and WOMEN WRITERS OF ENGLISH AND THEIR WORKS.

Editor's Note

My Introduction traces Twain's battle against "the Moral Sense" throughout the course of his writing career.

The Critical Extracts presented in this volume are numerous enough so that I wish to emphasize only a few of the interpretative high points.

The "Jumping Frog" story is shrewdly examined by James M. Cox, as is the "Carnival of Crime" tale by Robert Keith Miller.

"The Stolen White Elephant" is studied as parodistic art by Virginia S. Hale, while "The Man That Corrupted Hadleyburg" is socially contextualized by Susan K. Harris, and compared to *Paradise Lost* by Gary Scharnhorst.

Philip S. Foner stresses Twain's career as a social critic, and expounds "The £1,000,000 Note" as a revelation of Twain's bitter relationship with the world of high finance. Harold H. Kolb Jr. studies the development of Twain's tonalities.

Introduction

HAROLD BLOOM

The most useful critical study of Mark Twain, for me, remains James M. Cox's *Mark Twain: The Fate of Humor* (1966). Cox does not deal with the short stories but rather with Twain's major works, including *Adventures of Huckleberry Finn, Pudd'nhead Wilson, Roughing It,* and *Innocents Abroad.* It is Cox who points out that "Mark Twain" was a steamboat pilot's signal for danger, not for safe water. Samuel Clemens, who became Mark Twain, remains our leading humorist, but his best work—the short stories included—is replete with signals for danger. Cox emphasizes also the recurrence in Twain's writings of the figure of a Stranger— ironic and mysterious—whose interventions bring about danger, whether to the established moral order or to our universal lust for illusions.

Twain, in Cox's view, fought a lifelong campaign against the censorious conscience, the Freudian superego. A speculator by nature, Twain was a great escape artist, like his masterly creation, Huck Finn. The best of Twain's short stories are exercises in evasiveness, because the truth, as for Hamlet, is what kills us. The abyss of nihilism beckons as uncannily in Mark Twain as it does in Shakespeare, or in Nietzsche.

Twain's first artistic and commercial success was his early short story (1865), "The Celebrated Jumping Frog of Calaveras County," where the story-teller, Wheeler, is the ancestor of all the deadpan narrators who are the glory of Twain's style. Twain became one of the great performers of his age; his lectures, mock-solemnly delivered, vied in effectiveness with Emerson's visionary addresses and Dickens's dramatic readings. Wheeler's mode of narration became Twain's platform manner: disarmingly innocent and yet comically urgent.

In 1876, Twain read aloud, to a select Hartford audience, the outrageous "Facts Concerning the Recent Carnival of Crime in Connecticut," a fantasy in which the ironic dwarf, his Conscience, is destroyed by the narrator as prelude to beginning the world anew:

> I killed thirty-eight persons during the first two weeks—all of them on account of ancient grudges. I burned a dwelling that interrupted my view. I swindled a widow and some orphans out of their last cow . . .

The war against the superego is carried on much more indirectly in "The Stolen White Elephant" of 1882, where the parody of detective-fiction hyperbolically indicts what might be termed the investigative impulse itself. A fear of madness, at the root of Twain's genius for humor, translated into the superb story, "The Man That Corrupted Hadleyburg," a *Paradise Lost*-in-little, with intimations of Pre-Millennialism (1899). Hadleyburg, "the most honest and upright little town in all the region round about," could be anywhere in the United States as we again approach the Millennium. The man who "corrupts" it is an archetypal Mark Twain mysterious or ironic Stranger, a truth-seeking Satan. A small masterpiece in style and plot, the Fall of Hadleyburg may be Twain's finest victory over the hypocrisies of the societal element in the superego.

With "The £1,000,000 Note" of 1893, Twain refined his parable of corruption. Light as this story continues to be, it has few peers in its revelation of the illusions of finance. Nihilism, a Gnostic awareness of the illusiveness of both nature and society, attains its extreme of intensity in the posthumously published *Mysterious Stranger* fragments. Little Satan, Twain's final hero, indicts the superego or Moral Sense as the true villain of human existence. God, the deity of Moral Virtue akin to Blake's Urizen, is the final culprit, for Mark Twain. An attack upon God, however God is construed, is a very difficult basis for humor, as Twain realized. At the outer limits of his art, Twain yielded to despair. ✿

Biography of
Samuel Clemens (Mark Twain)
(1835–1910)

Samuel Langhorne Clemens, the man remembered today as Mark Twain, was born on November 30, 1835. He was the son of John M. and Jane L. Clemens of Florida, Missouri. In 1839, the Clemens family moved to Hannibal, Missouri; this area inspired the settings of many Twain stories. From 1840 until 1849, Samuel attended school regularly, but starting in 1847, he also held odd jobs, including work on several newspapers. After leaving school, Clemens continued his work in the newspaper trade, first as an apprentice and then as a full-time newspaperman and printer. In his free time, he became a riverboat pilot. When the Civil War broke out, his piloting career ended when he joined a battalion of Confederate irregulars. In post-war years, Clemens continued to work on gazettes and newspapers as he formalized the writing career for which he is renowned today.

After holding several different positions, by 1862, Clemens occupied a full-time position as a reporter and feature writer on the Virginia City *Territorial Enterprise.* In 1863, he used the pen name "Mark Twain" for the first time. The name is a homage to his days as a pilot; a "mark twain" stretch of river was two fathoms deep. Continuing his wandering life, Clemens moved again, this time to San Francisco where he met and worked for the editor Bret Harte. His career as a writer began to take shape when, in November of 1865, *The Saturday Press* in New York published "Jim Smiley and His Jumping Frog," the story that would later become "The Celebrated Jumping Frog of Calaveras County." In 1866, as a correspondent for the *Alta California*, Clemens traveled first to New York and later, in 1867, to Europe on a tour of the Mediterranean. During this voyage, Clemens met Olivia Langdon, his future wife. When he returned, Elisha Bliss, an editor from Hartford, Connecticut, suggested to him that he write a book about his European trip. That suggestion led to the writing of Twain's first book, *The Innocents Abroad,* which Bliss published in 1869. In the same year, Twain met William Dean Howell, who became his literary advisor, a post he would hold for some forty years.

Clemens joined the *Buffalo Express* as a part owner, due to the generosity of his future father-in-law, Jervis Langdon. Samuel Clemens and Olivia Langdon married on February 2, 1870, in Elmira, New York. Their first son, Langdon Clemens, was born on November 7, 1870. Then, late in 1871, Clemens and his new family moved to Hartford, Connecticut.

The following years were both busy and difficult ones for Mark Twain. Elisha Bliss published *Roughing It* for Twain in February of 1872, and the Clemens' first daughter, Olivia Susan, later called Susy, was born on March 19 of that year. But their infant son, Langdon, died of diphtheria just three months later. In 1874, a second daughter, Clara, was born. Clemens also started work on *The Adventures of Tom Sawyer* and adapted his work, *The Gilded Cage,* for the theater. In September of 1874, *The Gilded Cage* opened in New York and brought financial success to Twain. The *Atlantic Monthly* published "The Facts Concerning the Recent Carnival of Crime in Connecticut" in June of 1876. In the same year, Clemens began work on one of his most famous novels, *Huckleberry Finn,* and although Elisha Bliss finally published *The Adventures of Tom Sawyer* a year and a half after receiving the manuscript, Clemens considered changing publishers in hopes of encountering fewer delays. His relationship with Bret Harte also suffered despite collaborating with him on a new play, *Ah Sin.* When the play finally opened the following year in New York, it closed after only five weeks. Despite this, Clemens started writing *The Prince and the Pauper.*

In 1878, Twain traveled in Europe. After more than a year away, he published *The Tramp Abroad* in 1880 and continued his work on *Huckleberry Finn.* Jean, the fourth and last Clemens child, was born in July of 1880. To gain material for a book, Twain traveled on the Mississippi River, publishing *Life on the Mississippi* as a result. At the same time, Twain took a break from writing *Huckleberry Finn* and established the Charles L. Webster Publishing Company in an attempt to increase control over his books. A lecture tour with George Washington Cable, author and civil rights advocate, occupied much of his time in 1885, and in that year, he finished and published *The Adventures of Huckleberry Finn.*

Twain began writing *A Connecticut Yankee in King Arthur's Court* in 1886, the same year he took half ownership of the Paige Typesetter. His publishing company released the finished *Connecticut*

Yankee in December of 1889, when Twain secured all rights to the Paige Typesetter. In 1891, Twain moved his family to Europe to cut down on expenses since his Paige investment had soured. In 1894, the Charles L. Webster Publishing Company printed *Tom Sawyer Abroad*, but later that same year Twain was forced to declare bankruptcy. In the fall, the American Publishing Company published *Pudd'nhead Wilson*.

To pay his debts, Twain began a worldwide lecture tour in July of 1885, and while in England in 1896, he learned of the death of his daughter Susy from meningitis. In that same year, *Tom Sawyer, Detective* was published. By the beginning of 1898, Twain managed to pay off all his debts and was able to return to America by 1900.

His beloved wife Olivia died of heart disease in 1904, so Twain moved to an apartment on Fifth Avenue in New York. In the next several years, he received many honors, including an honorary Doctorate of Literature from Oxford University in 1907. His daughter Clara married in 1909, but tragedy struck the family again when Jean Clemens, who suffered from eplilepsy, died a few months after her sister's wedding. In the winter of 1910, Twain's health failed significantly, and on April 21, 1910, Samuel L. Clemens died. He was buried in Elmira, New York. ❈

Plot Summary of
"The Celebrated Jumping Frog
of Calaveras County"

This story originally appeared as "Jim Smiley and His Jumping Frog" in 1865; Mark Twain later made revisions to the text and published it, along with other short works, as *The Celebrated Jumping Frog of Calaveras County, and Other Sketches* in 1867. It is considered the story that established Twain's writing career.

"The Celebrated Jumping Frog of Calaveras County" is a "frame story," in which the narrator's story "frames" another narrative in the tale. As the story begins, the narrator visits a man named Simon Wheeler as a favor to a friend back in the East. His friend wants to know about another acquaintance, the Reverend Leonidas W. Smiley. Wheeler tells the narrator that he does not remember *Leonidas* Smiley, but he does know a *Jim* Smiley quite well. Wheeler then begins to tell Smiley's story. Thus the narrator's story about meeting Wheeler frames the raconteur's recollection of Jim Smiley.

Sometime around 1849 or 1850, apparently, Smiley lived in the same mining camp where the narrator found Wheeler. Smiley had a reputation as a person who could bet on anything and always come out the winner. His horse, which supposedly suffered from asthma, was referred to in jest as the "fifteen-minute nag." "[Smiley] used to win money on that horse." Wheeler explained to the narrator. "[S]he was so slow and always had the asthma, or the distemper, or the consumption, or something of that kind—but always at the fag end of the race she'd get excited and desperate-like." Smiley also had a bull pup named Andrew Jackson that spent most of its time sitting around. When there was money bet on the dog, however, Wheeler recalled that the dog became a fighting machine. Smiley also kept "rat-tarriers," chicken cocks, and tomcats, and would bet on all of them. He even bet one day on whether the ailing parson's wife would recover.

Smiley "ketched a frog one day, and took him home, and said he cal'klated to edercate him; so he never done nothing for three months but set in his back yard and learn that frog to jump." Smiley called the frog Dan'l Webster. The frog jumped so high and so well that it could catch a fly from a counter top, and Smiley soon won many bets because of Dan'l Webster.

One day, though, a stranger arrived in the mining camp and questioned the frog's abilities. Smiley was circumspect at first, not wanting to reveal too many details about his prize frog. But when the stranger insisted, Smiley placed a bet of $40 that his frog could outjump any frog in Calaveras County. The stranger said that he would match the bet, except that he did not have a frog to put up against Dan'l Webster. Wanting to take the bet, Smiley told the stranger he would find a frog for him in the nearby swamp, if the stranger was willing to wait and watch Dan'l Webster for him. The stranger quickly agreed.

In Smiley's absence, the stranger removed Dan'l Webster from his box and fed him teaspoonfuls of quail shot—metal pellets packed into a shotgun shell for hunting birds. When Smiley returned from the swamp with the other frog, the contest began, but Dan'l Webster didn't budge at Smiley's cue. According to Wheeler, the frog "was planted as solid as an anvil, and he couldn't no more stir than if he was anchored out." Smiley was understandably puzzled. The stranger took the money and left. When Smiley picked up his frog, he noticed how heavy the frog was. When Smiley turned the frog upside down, it "belched out a double handful of shot." A very angry Smiley dropped the frog and ran after the deceitful stranger.

At this point in the story, someone called Wheeler away, but he asked the narrator to wait for his return. When the narrator was about to leave, Wheeler came back. He started to tell the narrator about Smiley and his "yaller one-eyed cow that didn't have no tail" but the narrator could not endure any more. He said good-bye to the old fellow and left the mining camp. ❈

List of Characters in
"The Celebrated Jumping Frog
of Calaveras County"

Narrator: The speaker of the story is a man who is inquiring about the Rev. Leoindas W. Smiley. In response to his inquiry, Simon Wheeler tells the narrator stories about an acquaintence named Jim Smiley.

Simon Wheeler: The narrator who recounts the events in an old mining camp around 1850. Wheeler is bald, fat, and generally good-natured. While telling his story, he maintains a deadpan expression that adds to the comic tone of the tale.

Jim Smiley: The subject of Wheeler's story, Jim Smiley will take any bet—because of his uncommonly good luck, he usually wins. Smiley has many animals that he bets on—a horse, a fighting dog, chickens, and tomcats—but it is his jumping frog, Dan'l Webster, that is his favorite.

Dan'l Webster: Named for the noted statesman and orator of the day, this is the famous frog that Jim Smiley caught one day and trained to jump for three months. Smiley won many bets because of the frog's jumping ability.

The stranger: A nameless man outwits Smiley and wins the bet because he feeds Dan'l Webster quail shot before the contest, making the frog too heavy to jump. ❁

Critical Views on
"The Celebrated Jumping Frog
of Calaveras County"

James M. Cox on Being Taken In

[In this excerpt, Cox, the author of a 1966 analysis of Twain's humor, *Mark Twain: The Fate of Humor*, draws parallels between Smiley's being taken in by the shrewd stranger and the narrator's same fate at the hands of Simon Wheeler:]

While Mark Twain painfully condescends to suffer the boredom of listening to Wheeler's interminable narrative, Wheeler is apparently so absorbed in his own story that he is utterly unaware of his listener's attitude. He is, after all, the deadpan narrator; and if he suspects the condescension, he betrays no hint of his suspicion, being content to blockade Mark Twain and force him to undergo the role of listener.

This structure, revealing two contrasting styles, imitates the action of Wheeler's story. Smiley, who had consciously trained his animals, fostering their genius and lying in wait for gullible souls willing to bet on the merely natural animals to beat them, it "taken in" by a deadpan stranger. Innocently refusing to see the virtue of Smiley's frog, the mysterious stranger dupes him into fetching a mere ordinary, unpedigreed, and unnamed frog with which he defeats the celebrated Dan'l Webster. The stranger is not innocent, of course, but the first of a long line of mock-innocents to people Mark Twain's world, and his victory over Smiley comes by virtue of his having weighted Dan'l Webster with so much birdshot that the frog's incomparable style is reduced to no more than an impotent strain against its recently acquired sense of gravity. The stranger's secret act of "fixing" the jumping contest corresponds to the artist's "secret" structure which becomes apparent to the reader only after he has been taken in.

In much the same way the stranger's deadpan takes in Smiley, Wheeler's style is "taking in" the literary language which introduces it. The literary "Mark Twain" quite appropriately suspects that he has been taken in as he recounts the story, but he obtusely attributes the trick to his friend from the remote East, not to the beguiling Wheeler.

—James M. Cox, *Mark Twain: The Fate of Humor* (Princeton: Princeton University Press, 1966): pp. 28–29.

⊛

EVERETT EMERSON ON VICTIMIZATION OF SMILEY AND THE NARRATOR

[Like Cox, Emerson considers the duality of listeners and narrators in this section of his 1984 biographical study of Mark Twain. This extract concentrates on the theme of victimization—that is, Smiley the character as victim, as well as Twain, the narrator of the outer frame of "The Jumping Frog of Calaveras County," as an easy mark for Wheeler's deadpan narration:]

The version of Mark Twain's story that was published in the New York *Saturday Press* of November 18, 1865, is entitled "Jim Smiley and His Jumping Frog." (It had arrived too late for publication in *Artemus Ward, His Travels.*) Told with infinite care, the story is narrated by two tellers, Mark Twain, who introduces his account somewhat pompously, and Simon Wheeler, the garrulous vernacular storyteller who sets forth his story for Mark Twain's ears. Simon Wheeler, the erstwhile poet, was kin to Ben Coon of Angel's Camp, who (according to Mark Twain's 1897 account) had told him the story. The addition of a second narrator, carefully characterized, enriches the sketch greatly. There is irony in both tellings. Mark Twain pretends that he has had to put up with a preposterous bore as the result of Artemus Ward's request that he look up the Rev. Leonidas W. Smiley; and Simon Wheeler, whom he meets on his search, pretends that there is nothing funny about the story he tells in response. Wheeler possessed what Mark Twain had called in his 1864 sketch "'Mark Twain' in the Metropolis" "the first virtue of a comedian, which is to do funny things with grave decorum and without seeming to know that they are funny." Moreover, Wheeler's artfully told story appears to be never-ending and pointless. This double irony gives readers the pleasure of feeling superior to Mark Twain, the narrator, though an alert one sees that Mark Twain is playfully portraying himself as having been victimized.

That the technique of the story focuses attention on the narrator as victim is quite appropriate, since victimization is also a theme of the story. Jim Smiley, the optimistic and compulsive gambler, always looking for a little excitement, can be fooled by a stranger because he lacks the caution of the experienced Westerner. But before Simon Wheeler reveals Smiley's gullibility in the climax of the yarn, he creates great interest in the gambler, as well as in his animals, which are exaggerated to heroic proportions. [. . .]

As the story moves to its climax, the narration moves to drama, and we hear conversations between Jim and the stranger, whose coolheadedness more than matches Jim's studied indifference. Jim thinks he has entrapped the stranger when the latter observes, "I don't see no points about that frog that's any better'n any other frog." Jim's search for a frog for the stranger, to compete with Dan'l, provides the stranger with time to fill what was to become known as the celebrated jumping frog of Calaveras County "pretty near up to his chin" with quail-shot. Thus the stranger's frog is permitted to win, whereupon the winner comments, again cooly, "I don't see no points about that frog that's any better'n any other frog," and leaves.

It is Mark Twain's control of point of view that makes the story so rich. We see the narrator's view of Simon Wheeler, and Wheeler's view of Jim Smiley; each is consistent, and subtle.

—Everett Emerson, *The Authentic Mark Twain: A Literary Biography of Samuel L. Clemens* (Philadelphia: University of Pennsylvania Press, 1984): pp. 29, 30.

⊗

HENRY B. WONHAM ON TWAIN'S REVISIONS

[Henry Wonham is the author of *Mark Twain and the Art of the Tall Tale* (1993), a study of Twain's storytelling techniques that analyzes the evolution of Twain's style. In this extract, Wonham mentions the several drafts that Twain found to be necessary to produce "The Celebrated Jumping Frog of Calaveras County" as he wanted, and he concludes that Twain's rewriting enabled him to meld an oral tradition of storytelling with engaging textual narrative:]

In the third version, as it appeared in the New York *Saturday Press* on November 18, 1865, Mark Twain has been tricked into a rhetorical corner where he must endure Wheeler's "infernal reminiscence" of the "infamous" Jim Smiley. According to Joseph Twichell, Twain pigeonholed the first two drafts because he found them "poor and flat." He preferred the third because in it the relationship between the garrulous Simon Wheeler and his impatient, unappreciative auditor locates the tale within a specific context of performance. His revision added nothing either to the substance of Wheeler's tale or to the yarn spinner's easygoing narrative style. What Twain sought after two false starts was a plausible and realistic drama of performance through which to relate the fictional storyteller to his fictional listener in such a way that the reader enjoys "the spontaneity of a personal relation, which is the very essence of interest."

Twain's early development of methods for effectively conveying oral yarns in print involved no magical breakthrough, and he would likely have been the first to point out that his early success as a literary yarn spinner owed a great deal to the methods of previous humorists. But the jumping frog story was unprecedented in its manner of blending the concreteness of a storytelling performance, as described by the pedantic realist Mark Twain, with the fantastic imagery and illogic of a very different kind of narrative creator, Simon Wheeler. It is the drama that unfolds between these two competing imaginations, and the contrast between their chosen media, that fuels the sketch with interest and ignites its satire. Bernard DeVoto made a similar point when he described the essential method of Mark Twain's humor by pointing to the interplay of fantasy and reality in "Jim Baker's Blue-Jay Yarn." Baker's winged friends, with their unexpectedly refined qualities of intellect and emotion, are the "monstrous fabrications" of Baker's active imagination. Yet the old miner himself, according to DeVoto, "is creation from the world of reality. He lives, and no fantasy has gone into his creation, but only the sharp perception of an individual." "Fantasy," DeVoto concludes, "is thus an instrument of realism and the humor of Mark Twain merges into the fiction that is his highest reach."

> —Henry B. Wonham, *Mark Twain and the Art of the Tall Tale.* (New York: Oxford University Press, 1993): p. 68.

⚘

STUART HUTCHINSON ON LANGUAGE IN "THE CELEBRATED JUMPING FROG"

[Stuart Hutchinson, author of *Mark Twain: Humour on the Run* (1994) believes that language serves to accentuate differences in Twain's stories: East-West, stranger-native, Old World-New World, happy-sad. In his extract, Hutchinson finds Twain's gift in this manipulation of opposites based on exaggerated renderings of the vernacular:]

Twain obviously enjoys Simon Wheeler's vernacular tale of Jim Smiley and his frog. He delights in being able to do Wheeler's language and expects us to be delighted by the language. Nor is the narrator taken in by the "westerner," Simon Wheeler, who tells Smiley's story to the narrator. It is rather the narrator's friend in the East who takes the narrator in, by setting him up to hear Wheeler. Presumably the friend wants the fun of it, though the narrator himself is only bored "to death" by the result. He walks out on Wheeler, when we might like him to stay. Many of us would love to hear Wheeler's account of Smiley's "yaller one-eyed cow that didn't have no tail, just a short stump like a bannanner."

As the name indicates, Smiley is where happiness may be found. He is unburdened beyond the dreams of Thoreau at Walden: "he never done nothing for three months but set in his backyard and learn that frog to jump." Smiley "most always come out winner," because he was not bothered if he lost. Though he is eventually deceived by the "stranger," it has no lasting effect on him. After his dog, there was the frog; after the frog, the cow; after the cow. . . .

Smiley's happiness in the West is apparently invulnerable, even in defeat. This happiness is true liberation, but not everyone can find it even in the West. The "stranger" who outsmarts Smiley has not found it. He is the begetter of a long line of strangers in Twain. Their function, for good or ill, is to disturb and even destroy faith or illusion. As a consequence, the strangers themselves may be left the poorer, as was sometimes the narrator in *The Innocents Abroad*. He was the stranger in the Old World, mocking beliefs which could not be his, and experiencing triumph diluted with loss. He shares the sadness we find in the stranger in the "Jumping Frog" story:

> And the feller studies a minute and then says, kinder sad-like, "Well, I'm only a stranger here and I ain't got no frog; but if I had a frog, I'd bet you."

This sad tone is used to set Smiley up, but it is also the tone of a cynic, saddened by the knowledge that he must always poison delight.

—Stuart Hutchinson, *Mark Twain: Humour on the Run.* (Amsterdam: Rodophi, 1994): pp. 38–39.

Plot Summary of
"Facts Concerning the Recent Carnival of Crime in Connecticut"

Originally published in 1876, "Facts Concerning the Recent Carnival of Crime in Connecticut" opens with the narrator's description of pleasure at reading a letter from a favorite relative, Aunt Mary, announcing an impending visit. The mere sight of her letter brings back fond memories and causes the narrator such a general feeling of satisfaction and contentment that he states: "If my most pitiless enemy could appear before me at this moment, I would freely right any wrong I may have done him."

No sooner has the narrator finished this statement when the door opens and an ugly dwarf walks in. The dwarf stands about two feet tall and his misshapen body is covered with a green mold like that of mildewed bread. Without any introduction, the dwarf makes himself comfortable by grabbing the narrator's pipe and then demanding a match. The narrator is both indignant and embarrassed at the same time. He notices a faint resemblance between the dwarf and himself, and the creature's bad behavior reminds the narrator of himself in private. When the narrator tries to scold the dwarf for his bad manners, he immediately receives a series of reprimands: for turning away a tramp, for lying, and for refusing to read a woman's manuscript. All of these events occurred very recently in the narrator's life, and he reacts painfully: "Remorse! Remorse! . . . Every sentence was an accusation, and every accusation was a truth."

To make matters worse, the dwarf then rebukes the narrator for transgressions that he committed in the past. The discomfort on the narrator's face at the recital of this litany of sins causes the dwarf considerable contentment. Then the dwarf begins to describe an uncharitable thought the narrator had while dreaming. At this, the narrator says that to know his inner thoughts and dreams, the dwarf must be the devil, at which point the dwarf clarifies that he is, in fact, the narrator's Conscience.

When the narrator tries to grab the creature by the throat, the dwarf eludes his grasp by leaping up. "Folly! Lightening does not move more quickly than my Conscience did! He darted aloft so suddenly that in the moment my fingers clutched the empty air he was already perched on the top of the high bookcase, with his thumb at his nose in token of derision," says the narrator. At this point, the speaker's son enters the room. In his excitement and confusion, the narrator yells at his son to leave immediately. Only after the boy leaves does the narrator realize that the dwarf is visible to him alone. With this realization, the narrator decides to be nice to the dwarf and to trick him. But the dwarf is far too clever to fall for this. When asked why he is now visible, the dwarf responds that it is the narrator's own fault since he called the dwarf when he referred to his "most pitiless enemy." He insists that he is the narrator's master. The dwarf is quite content to be visible because, as he explains, he can look the narrator in the eye and can insult him to his face.

When the narrator asks if a Conscience has a purpose in harassing its subject, the dwarf responds that there is no honest intent in his actions, he is merely doing his job: "We simply do it because it is 'business' . . . The purpose of it *is* to improve man, but *we* are merely disinterested agents." The dwarf further explains that as a Conscience he follows orders from a higher authority, but, he admits, at times, he and other Consciences may exert extra effort in harassing their charges just for the pleasure of it. But then the narrator complains that no matter what action he may take, his Conscience bothers him. He demands that the dwarf tell him how to satisfy his Conscience. To wit, the dwarf responds: "I don't care *what* act you may turn your hand to, I can straightaway whisper a word in your ear and make you think you have committed a dreadful meanness. It is my *business*—and my joy—to make you repent."

Their conversation shifts to the dwarf's size and appearance. The narrator says that he is thankful for the dwarf's invisibility, because its outer aspect is so unpleasant. Quickly, the dwarf places the blame for his nasty appearance squarely on the narrator's shoulders. He claims that when the narrator was a boy of nine, his Conscience was "seven feet high, and as pretty as a picture," but as the narrator began to rebel against his Conscience, the dwarf gradually lost stature and gained his present tough and ugly exterior. The rebellious nature of the narrator even has the effect of inducing sleep in the dwarf. The narrator insists on knowing more about the relationship of action to size. When he questions the dwarf about other people's consciences, the dwarf tells him that his neighbor's conscience, once tall and faultless, is now so small that it sleeps in a cigar box, while the conscience of a boyhood friend is now thirty-seven feet high. The dwarf cited other examples: Aunt Mary's conscience cannot find a door large enough to let her pass, whereas the conscience of the narrator's editor, recently on exhibition, required a microscope to see.

As the dwarf is speaking, Aunt Mary bursts into the room. After exchanging joyful greetings with her nephew, she begins to scold him because of a promise that he made but never kept. When she reminded him that he had agreed long ago to help a family, but never had, the narrator felt pains of guilt go through him. When he looked up at the dwarf, he discovered that his Conscience was also feeling the effect of this guilt. As Aunt Mary continues her reprimand and describes the horrible situations that this family had faced because of her nephew's neglect, the dwarf suffers more and more visibly, appearing about to faint. Unable to take any more, the dwarf falls to the floor in pain, and at this, the narrator jumps up and locks the door.

Aunt Mary stared in confusion and asked her nephew to explain his actions. As the narrator behaves more and more bizarrely in front of his aunt, she chides him all the more harshly, not knowing how the weight of her words are bearing down on the dwarf. When, at last, the dwarf can withstand no more, he falls asleep. The narrator leaps at him, tearing the dwarf to shreds and throwing the pieces into the blazing fire.

The narrator, at last, is free of his Conscience. He shouts at his aunt: "You behold before you a man whose life-conflict is done, whose soul is at peace; dead to remorse; a man WITHOUT A CONSCIENCE!" Faced with her nephew's hysteria, Aunt Mary runs away. In the following two weeks, the narrator kills thirty-eight people, swindles a widow out of her money, burns down a building, and generally enjoys himself as never before. The narrator ends his tale with an open advertisement to all medical schools looking for cadavers: as a favor to the narrator, they could clear out the dead bodies in the narrator's basement for him before seeking bodies elsewhere. ❁

List of Characters in
"Facts Concerning the Recent Carnival
of Crime in Connecticut"

The narrator: Speaking with a drawl, the prosperous middle-aged writer-narrator tells about a visit by an ugly dwarf that changed the course of his life. The narrator must grapple with the facts that the dwarf represents his Conscience, that no one else can see the dwarf except him, and that the dwarf has come to tell him some painful truths. In the end, the narrator kills his Conscience; this frees him to live without guilt from the consequences of his actions.

Aunt Mary: The very moral and proper aunt of the narrator. Although his childhood memories of her are fond ones, the narrator clearly remembers that his aunt reminds him about moral duties in life.

The dwarf: About the same age as the narrator, the dwarf—the narrator's Conscience—is about two feet tall, very ugly, and covered by green moss. He is invisible to all except the narrator. The dwarf can leap about the room when necessary. He reveals to the narrator the very unpleasant consequences that await those who ignore their consciences. An overwhelming burden of guilt, brought on by the narrator's Aunt Mary, causes the dwarf to fall asleep, at which point the narrator destroys his Conscience. ❀

Critical Views on
"Facts Concerning the Recent Carnival of Crime in Connecticut"

ALBERT BIGELOW PAINE ON THE RECEPTION
OF "CARNIVAL OF CRIME"

[Albert Bigelow Paine wrote one of the best biographies of Mark Twain in 1912, two years after the author's death. He is also known for his reworking of an unfinished Twain manuscript into what was later called "The Mysterious Stranger, A Romance" (1916). In this excerpt from his distinguished three-volume biography (reprinted by Chelsea House, 1997), Paine describes the events at the Monday Evening Club when Twain first read the "Carnival of Crime" to his colleagues. As Paine notes, the tale was received warmly for its vividness of character:]

Once that winter the Monday Evening Club met at Mark Twain's home, and instead of the usual essay he read them a story: "The Facts Concerning the Recent Carnival of Crime in Connecticut." It was the story of a man's warfare with a personified conscience—a sort of "William Wilson" idea, though less weird, less somber, and with more actuality, more verisimilitude. It was, in fact, autobiographical, a setting-down of the author's daily self-chidings. The climax, where conscience is slain, is a startling picture which appeals to most of humanity. So vivid is it all, that it is difficult in places not to believe in the reality of the tale, though the allegory is always present.

The club was deeply impressed by the little fictional sermon. One of its ministerial members offered his pulpit for the next Sunday if Mark Twain would deliver it to his congregation. Howells welcomed it for the *Atlantic,* and published it in June. It was immensely successful at the time, though for some reason it seems to be little known or remembered today. Now and then a reader mentions it, always with enthusiasm. Howells referred to it repeatedly in his letters, and finally persuaded Clemens to let Osgood bring it out, with "A True Story," in dainty, booklet form. If the reader does not already know the tale, it will pay him to look it up and read it, and then to read it again.

—Albert Bigelow Paine, *Mark Twain: A Biography* (New York: Harper & Brothers, 1912): p. 569. ☙

[Duality is a repeating theme in Twain criticism. In this extract from Susan Gillman's 1989 book on Twain, *Dark Twins: Imposture and Identity in Mark Twain's America*, quotes from Twain's notebook are used to establish his views on the duality of detectives and criminals, and equate these views with characters such as the dwarf in "Facts Concerning the Recent Carnival of Crime in Connecticut":]

The relationship between detective and mystery meant more to Twain, though, than simply a representation of external social control; it also stood as a model for an internalized power struggle in which the criminal, antisocial self is constantly threatening the control of selfhood willed by the socialized self. As far back as 1877, Twain remembers, he had experimented with this detective-criminal model of the doubled psyche in "Facts Concerning the Recent Carnival of Crime in Connecticut":

> That was an attempt to account for our seeming *duality*—the presence in us of another *person*; not a slave of ours, but free and independent and with a character distinctly its own. I made my conscience that other person and it came before me in the form of a malignant dwarf and told me plain things about myself and shamed me and scoffed at me and derided me. This creature was so much its own master that it would leave the premises . . . and go off on a spree with other irresponsible consciences—and discuss their masters (no–their slaves).

Like Huck's "deformed conscience" internally berating him in the linguistic pieties of the dominant culture, Twain's dwarf serves as no ethical guide but instead dominates as an alien "creature" invading from without, as "master" to Twain's "slave." But the precise structure of roles in this internal power struggle eludes Twain, just as the division of power between the dreamer and his dream-artist ("the mysterious mental magician who is here not our slave, but only our guest") does in "My Platonic Sweetheart."

The conception of duality in "Carnival of Crime" as a conscious power struggle was "a crude attempt to work out the duality idea," Twain asserted later in 1898, in both his notebook and the "Sweetheart" story. By this time "Carnival" appeared lacking, especially in comparison to Robert Louis Stevenson's version of a similar duality (presented with "genius and power") in Dr. Jekyll and Mr. Hyde

(1886). Stevenson's book was "nearer, yes, but not near enough" to Twain's own developing theory, he explained in his notebook: "J. & H. were the dual persons in one body, quite distinct in nature and character . . . the falsity being the ability of the one person to step into the other's place, *at will.*" Stevenson was wrong, Twain says, just as he himself was wrong "in the beginning" to theorize the conscience as man's conscious tormentor. On the contrary, "distinct duality" is unconscious: "The two persons in a man do not even *know* each other and . . . have never even suspected each other's existence." Twain's "*new* notion" of duality, then, led away from literary conceptions derived from popular fiction and toward contemporary experimentation in America and Europe with hypnosis, hysteria, thought transference, and dream analysis—all apparent avenues to the unconscious.

> —Susan Gillman, *Dark Twins: Imposture and Identity in Mark Twain's America* (Chicago: University of Chicago Press, 1989): pp. 45–46.

⊛

GLADYS CARMEN BELLAMY ON TWAIN'S BURLESQUE

[Gladys Carmen Bellamy is a well-known Twain scholar, whose works include *Mark Twain as a Literary Artist* (1950). In this extract, Bellamy categorizes "Facts Concerning the Recent Carnival of Crime in Connecticut" as typical of Twain's burlesque, stressing that in this tale Twain concentrates most on the folly of the human mind:]

Whether Mark Twain burlesques fashion reviews or inane question-and-answer departments or maudlin sob stories or sensational journalism, one thing is clear: it is the fatuity of the human mind that he parodies. He insists that the very faults of "Johnny Skae's Item" should most endear it to the public. In these literary caricatures the human intellect is held up to scorn in a scathing derision that applies to both writers and readers. He exhibits in his calculated burlesques that profound stupidity or laziness of men which leads them to accept such imperfect modes.

"The Recent Carnival of Crime in Connecticut" he labeled as "an exasperating metaphysical question . . . in the disguise of a literary extravaganza." This short study of the human conscience he had written in two days; but, as he wrote to Howells, he later spent three more days "trimming, altering, and working at it. I shall put in one more day's polishing on it." This is contrary to the accepted belief that he was either careless in revision or shunned it altogether. Howells felt that Hawthorne or Bunyan "might have been proud to imagine that powerful allegory, which had a grotesque force beyond either of them." Yet the sketch shows little variance in humorous technique from many other Mark Twain sketches. All the trimming, altering, and polishing were doubtless designed, as usual, to deliver a moral lesson "with telling force through the insidious medium of a travesty," to quote once more his own words explaining his practice in writing humor.

—Gladys Carmen Bellamy, *Mark Twain as a Literary Artist* (Norman: University of Oklahoma Press, 1950): pp. 34–35.

⊛

Robert Keith Miller on Twain's Growth as an Author

[In this extract from his 1983 book on Mark Twain, Robert Miller compares "Carnival of Crime" with "The Celebrated Jumping Frog of Calaveras County." Miller places the story in a chronological context with Twain's major works, *The Adventures of Tom Sawyer* and *Huckleberry Finn*, and with the Civil War short story, "The Private History of a Campaign That Failed":]

"The Jumping Frog" and "The Carnival of Crime" are both tall tales in the tradition of the American Southwest. But comparing the two stories reveals Twain's growth. For the most part, "The Jumping Frog" reflects an uncritical acceptance of local mores. The author is at ease within the culture that gave him his subject; there is no hint of Mark Twain as a social philosopher. In "The Carnival of Crime," however, we find Twain beginning to take issue with values his contemporaries held sacred. His attack upon conscience may be oblique, but it is nonetheless subversive. With the publication of this story, Twain "began to pit himself in imaginative opposition to the respectable community whose mores he had so eagerly adopted at the beginning of the '70s and whose approval he had so anxiously cultivated," as Kenneth Lynn has pointed out.

"The Facts Concerning the Recent Carnival of Crime in Connecticut" was published the same year as *The Adventures of Tom Sawyer.* Much of the next decade would be devoted to the composition of *Huckleberry Finn.* It was published in 1885, and in that same year, Twain wrote a fictionalized memoir, which is one of the best of his shorter works, "The Private History of a Campaign That Failed." At a time when the public revered the men who had fought in the Civil War and might take their pick from dozens of memoirs chronicling the glories of war, Twain chose to challenge such values—not by playing the fool in the relative safety of burlesque, but by offering a quietly realistic account of boy-soldiers off the battlefield.

—Robert Keith Miller, *Mark Twain* (New York: Frederick Ungar Publishing, 1983): pp. 164–165.

MAXWELL GEISMAR ON THE STORY'S INFLUENCE ON TWAIN'S LATER WORKS

[Maxwell Geismar's books include *Writers in Crisis: The American Novel, 1925–1940, Henry James and the Jacobites,* and *Mark Twain: An American Prophet.* He has also edited collections of short stories by Ring Lardner, Thomas Wolfe, and Jack London. In his analysis of "Facts Concerning the Recent Carnival of Crime in Connecticut," Geismar attributes this short story to opening the way for later works by Twain, such as *Pudd'nhead Wilson,* "The Man That Corrupted Hadleyburg," and "The Mysterious Stranger." According to Geismar, Twain's theory of the dark duality of self comes through most in this tale and its successors:]

Reprinted in Twain's collected works as "The Facts Concerning the Recent Carnival of Crime in Connecticut," this story was actually the prelude to a dark line of surrealistic parables which would include *Pudd'nhead Wilson*, "The Man That Corrupted Hadleyburg," and *The Mysterious Stranger*, in a different and more complex vein of Clemens' talent. Here we meet "the shriveled, shabby dwarf" who is about forty years old and no more than two feet high—this little person who is a deformity as a whole, "a vague, general, evenly blended, nicely adjusted deformity." And yet, "this vile bit of human rubbish seemed to bear a sort of remote and ill-defined resemblance to me!" He knows everything that goes on in the narrator's (Clemens') mind and spirit; he knows all his lies, vices, and sins, his arrogance, dishonesty, faithlessness, disloyalty, fits of violent anger, remorse. Clemens paints a very low view of himself here, and it is recognizable, until the narrator suddenly accuses his tormentor of being the devil, of being Satan himself. In this dubious shifting light, Clemens stresses his lifelong affinity with the fallen angel. But the odious and moldy dwarf turns out to be not the devil or Satan at all, but Twain's *conscience*.

And while the autobiographical narrator of the story is being roundly abused by his Conscience, he in turn abuses his Conscience and is intent upon capturing and killing the malignant dwarf. "Dwarf," as the dwarf explains, because while originally he started out precisely as tall as Clemens, his being neglected and abused through the years has steadily reduced his stature and power. [...]

Now in orthodox Freudian terms this story is just what it sounds like, and orthodox Freudians can shake their heads sadly and commiserate ad nauseam over poor Sam Clemens' burden of sin and guilt. In Rankian cultural terms, however, what this story marks (as Clemens must have felt and known in his depths) is the hero's liberation from the repressive burden of civilizational discontents, his defiance of conventional morality, his determination to be himself at all costs (every artist's design)—and hence, the "bliss, unalloyed bliss," of Clemens' natural spirit, and the carnival of crime which is the organism's realization it is enjoying itself despite the dictates of society.—A kind of vestigial guilt, yes, which is laughing at itself. This curious parable, so much harped upon by conventional depth psychology, proves to be the exact opposite, or the true rationale of art and the artist. This was Sam Clemens exorcising his Puritan past.

—Maxwell Geismar, *Mark Twain: An American Prophet* (Boston: Houghton Mifflin Company, 1970): pp. 51, 53. ✐

Plot Summary of
"The Stolen White Elephant"

This spoof on detective stories originally published in 1882 begins as a tale told by an elderly gentleman. The man explains that the King of Siam had offered a present to the Queen to offer an apology for a misguided border dispute. The narrator was put in charge of delivering the present, a white elephant, via a special ship outfitted just for this purpose. When the ship docked in New York harbor, the gentleman decided to give everyone, especially the elephant, some time off before continuing the journey, so he made arrangements for the elephant to be boarded in Jersey City. Two weeks passed without incident—until the elephant was discovered to be missing. The narrator explained that after receiving a call in the middle of the night reporting that someone had stolen the elephant, he flew to New York to seek help from the city's chief of detectives, Inspector Blunt.

The narrator's first impression of the police chief was very positive. Blunt was of compact size and had the habit of "knitting his brows and tapping his forehead reflectively with his finger." On reporting the crime to the detective, the narrator thought that the police chief showed no special reaction, as if the disappearance of a white elephant were a common event. But after reflecting quietly for a few minutes, Blunt announced: "This is no ordinary case. Every step must be warily taken . . . And secrecy must be observed—secrecy profound and absolute. Speak to no one about the matter, even the reporters. I will take care of *them*." The detective then proceeded to solicit specific and detailed information about the missing elephant. He questioned the narrator about the elephant's name, place of birth, parents, and physical description. As the narrator answered, the detective wrote down all the details. When Blunt was finished with his questions, he read back all the information so that the narrator could confirm its accuracy.

Once finished, Blunt called his assistant, a young man named Alaric. He ordered Alaric to make 50,000 copies of the elephant's description. He also told Alaric to have 50,000 copies of the elephant's photograph made the following morning. The copies, Blunt instructed, were to be sent to "every detective office and pawnbroker's shop on the continent."

The next item on Blunt's agenda was the reward. He told the narrator that a reward was necessary and suggested that $25,000 as a starting amount. Blunt then concentrated his inquiries on what food the elephant ate. When the narrator explained that the elephant would eat anything, Blunt insisted on more details. After noting which editions of the Bible and the number of men per day the elephant would prefer to eat, and the number of barrels of liquid the elephant would need to drink, Blunt summoned another detective so he could issue orders to his staff. Blunt sent some to shadow the elephant and others to follow the thieves. He sent men to watch the railroads, contacted the harbor police, placed detectives in the telegraph offices, and even sent others as far away as Canada. When the narrator left the detective's office that evening, he felt much relieved because he was confident that Blunt was a detective completely worthy of his trust and admiration.

By the next morning, news of the stolen white elephant has appeared in all the newspapers. Coverage of the story even includes eleven conflicting theories, offered by different detectives, on who the criminals are and how the crime was committed. What all the accounts have in common is that the most important opinion is Chief Inspector Blunt's.

The narrator returned to Blunt's office to encourage his continuing efforts to find the elephant, and asked about the newspapers' breaking the inspector's strategy of secrecy. Blunt responded that being in the public eye is essential for any detective. He added: "We must constantly show the public what we are doing, or they will believe we are doing nothing. It is much pleasanter to have a newspaper say, 'Inspector Blunt's ingenious and extraordinary theory is as follows' than to have it say some harsh thing, or, worse still, some sarcastic one." This impresses the narrator, and he turns over funds to cover the reward and expenses. Later, the narrator noticed in one newspaper that the reward is offered only to detectives. Blunt has no problem with this arrangement, telling the narrator that even if a common citizen found the elephant this would happen only after having followed "clews" stolen from a detective.

Soon, telegrams from all points began arriving. Many contained comments and descriptions like this one:

Just arrived. This village in consternation. Elephant passed through here at five in the morning. . . . He killed a horse; have secured a piece of it for a clew. Killed it with his trunk; from style of blow, think he struck it lefthanded. . . .

Hawes, Detective

With the arrival of each telegram, the narrator became more confused and discouraged. Blunt, on the other hand, was inspired and shouted out orders for more men to intensify the hunt. Among the other telegrams was one from P. T. Barnum, the circus impresario, offering to purchase the elephant for $4,000. Blunt sent a reply demanding $7,000, to which Barnum agreed. Several other telegrams followed, all originating from different locations, all reporting elephant sightings. With each, Blunt dispatched more men and issued more orders. But a thick fog rolled in at the end of the day, which stopped any more telegrams and greatly impeded further searching.

As the news of the search for the stolen white elephant spreads, even more, wilder, theories are generated in the newspapers. Along with the theories, however, is coverage of the wake of terror and confusion that the elephant has left during its travels. Although Inspector Blunt is pleased with the coverage, the narrator becomes even more despondent. He felt personally responsible for all the death and damage being attributed to the animal: "Sixty persons had been killed, and two hundred and forty wounded. All the accounts bore just testimony to the activity and devotion of the detectives, and all closed with the remark that 'three hundred thousand citizens and four detectives saw the dread creature, and two of the latter he destroyed.'" Then, with the fog, the elephant sightings dropped off significantly. Several days passed and on the urgings of Inspector Blunt, the narrator doubled the reward.

After two weeks without any new appearances by the elephant, Inspector Blunt suggested raising the reward to $75,000. The narrator did so, but the newspapers were becoming bored by the lack of news and started running caricatures of the detectives. Blunt, to the admiration of the narrator, stood firm.

Three weeks after the crime, the Inspector proposed a new plan to the elephant's discouraged caretaker. Blunt suggested that they compromise with the robbers by offering $100,000. When the narrator objected on the grounds that the overworked detectives would be left out in such a compromise, Blunt explained that in such an arrangement the detectives always got half. So, they proceeded with the new plan in which Blunt sent letters to the wives of the two criminals he had publicly associated with the theft of the elephant. Both wrote back nasty responses that Blunt ignored. He then put a completely unreadable advertisement in the next day's paper, assuring the dejected narrator that the thief would not only understand but would surely respond to it at midnight the following evening.

When the narrator returned with the money on the evening of the next day, he found a jubilant Inspector Blunt. Blunt escorted the old gentlemen to the basement of the police headquarters. In a darkened corner, the narrator stumbled over a huge mass—the elephant's dead body. Back in Blunt's office, there was general celebration. The reward money was distributed, champagne bottles were opened, and all present congratulated Blunt on his success. The next day the newspapers once again sang the praises of all detectives.

At the end of his story, the old gentleman has been ruined both financially and in his reputation. He not only lost the elephant for his government but $142,000 of his own money as well during the search to recover it. Despite this, his admiration for Blunt as the greatest detective has never faltered. ❁

List of Characters in
"The Stolen White Elephant"

The narrator: This man has been given the responsibility of delivering an elephant, a gift from the King of Siam, to England. In the tale he recounts Inspector Blunt's investigation that takes place after the elephant is stolen. As a result of the theft, the narrator, in the end, loses more than just the elephant.

Inspector Blunt: The Chief of New York's detectives, Blunt "cleverly" manages the search for the stolen elephant by calling in his best detectives. He regularly gives the narrator progress reports, while emphasizing the great expense that is being spent to find the animal, thus encouraging the narrator to offer greater and greater rewards. In the end, Blunt finds the elephant carcass, divides the reward with all his detectives, and keeps a healthy share for himself.

Jumbo: The narrator, during his first interview with Blunt, describes the missing elephant in detail. With all the publicity surrounding the case, even P. T. Barnum becomes interested in the fate of the elephant.

Alaric: Blunt's assistant who, on orders from the inspector, distributes 50,000 copies of the animal's description to every detective and pawnbroker in the general area. ❀

Critical Views on
"The Stolen White Elephant"

HOWARD G. BAETZHOLD ON THE
MODEL FOR INSPECTOR BLUNT

[Howard G. Baetzhold is a professor of English at Butler University. In this extract, he says that Mark Twain was probably writing a parody of detective Allan Pinkerton, the founder of a national detective agency, and compares Inspector Blunt's overconfident attitude with that found in the characters of Pinkerton's books:]

What seems to have irked Clemens most was the assumption of infallibility implied in the badge and motto, and in Pinkerton's books themselves. One passage in *The Mollie Maguires and the Detectives,* which appeared sometime during the summer of 1877, if he had read it, would have seemed an epitome of the attitude. With the case solved, Pinkerton quotes, with obvious relish, a statement by one of the prosecutors which could have been written by Inspector Blunt himself. Warning all thieves of the futility of flight, the prosecutor proclaims: "There is not a place on the habitable globe that these men can find refuge. . . . Let them go to the Rocky Mountains. . . . Let them transverse the bleak deserts of Siberia, penetrate into the jungles of India, or wander over the wild steppes of Central Asia, and they will be dogged and tracked and brought to justice. . . . The cat that holds the mouse in her grasp sometimes lets it go for a little while to play; but she knows well that at her will she can again have it secure within her claws; and Pinkerton's Agency may sometimes permit a man to believe that he is free who does not know that he may be traveling five thousand miles in the company of those whose vigilance never slumbers and whose eyes are never closed in sleep."

Blunt's name, which obviously reflects on his perceptiveness rather than any sort of gruffness, suggests that of George H. Bangs, head of Pinkerton's New York Agency. But otherwise Inspector Blunt was Mark Twain's very model of immodest Allan Pinkerton. From the outset the burlesque reflects Pinkerton's insistence on system, his allegedly keen cerebrations, and his supreme confidence. And Blunt's operation closely follows typical procedures of "the Chief."

As Franklin Rogers has aptly summarized them, Pinkerton's method involved "the accumulation of exhaustive details, both relevant and irrelevant, the constant surveillance of the suspect by detectives in disguise, and the securing of a confession by gaining the confidence of the suspect." Over and over again in his books "the Chief" tells of dispatching detectives with orders to send back voluminous reports, including all manner of gossip, family histories, the movement of suspects, drawings, measurements—anything, trivial or not, that might conceivably be related to the crime. Everyone possibly connected with the case was "shadowed." The number of operatives must have been astounding, and the cost immense. Although there is no question that the thoroughness of Pinkerton's methods often brought results, his stories reveal that there must have been much wasted money and effort.

> —Howard G. Baetzhold, "Of Detectives and Their Derring-Do: The Genesis of Mark Twain's 'The Stolen White Elephant.'" *Studies in American Humor* 2, no. 3 (January 1976): pp. 192–93.

VIRGINIA S. HALE ON TWAIN'S SATIRE OF DETECTIVE PRACTICES

[Virginia Hale, a professor of medieval studies at the University of Hartford, analyzes Twain's parody of the detective genre, emphasizing the outrageous excesses that he employed when writing "The Stolen White Elephant":]

A fascination with ratiocination helps to explain why Twain took up the detective story both in earnest: *Tom Sawyer, Detective* and *Pudd'nhead Wilson;* and as a satiric vehicle: *The Stolen White Elephant,* the *Double Barreled Detective Story,* and the incomplete *Simon Wheeler, Detective.*

In 1896, when Twain had just sold the collection which features *Tom Sawyer, Detective* and was apparently at work on two or possibly three of the others, his notebook contains the following remark: What a curious thing a detective story is. And was there ever one the author needn't be ashamed of except *Murders in the Rue Morgue?"*

The entry is followed by an outline for what may have been *Tom Sawyer's Conspiracy* or *Simon Wheeler, Detective*. So we are confronted with yet another of those paradoxes in Mark Twain: a sort of love-hate relationship, this time with a genre. It is a genre not altogether easy to define because, in truth, Twain was interested in two contemporary popular written forms: detective 'not-fiction' as well as fiction.

In *The Stolen White Elephant*, Twain parodies the practices of the Pinkertons in a mode which David Slaone would come to call Barnumesque. The parody is extravagant and, in the judgement of most modern readers, excessive. To summarize the story briefly: as a peace offering, The King of Siam sends a white elephant to the Queen of England. The narrator, a civil servant, is charged with its delivery, but the elephant is stolen. The fellow at once enlists the help of a detective force. (We know it is the Pinkertons because they wear a badge with a wide staring eye inscribed "*We Never Sleep.*") Chief Inspector Blunt takes over the case, employing a number of operatives without any success. After two weeks, Blunt pays the thieves a huge amount of money in exchange for information on the whereabouts of the elephant. They direct him to the elephant's decaying carcass, which lies in the basement of detective headquarters at the back of the room where 60 operatives sleep. Inspector Blunt exclaims, "Our noble profession is vindicated, here is your elephant." The narrator, having been financially ruined and politically disgraced, nevertheless professes tremendous admiration for the man he sees as "the greatest detective the world has yet produced." Though Twain stretches the satire to the breaking point, one cannot help being amused, for example, at the methodical development of the necessary profile of the missing elephant, including such details as length of trunk and length of tusks and the fact that the elephant "has a small scar in his left armpit" caused by a boil. We also learn he was an only child.

As outrageous as this appears, anyone acquainted with the detective stories of Allan Pinkerton will see this passage as gentle mockery indeed. According to Franklin Rogers:

> A Pinkerton investigation was an expensive procedure. At the outset of a case, Pinkerton's standard move was to dispatch one or more operatives to the scene of the crime. These men would go in disguise, and at least one would pose as a person wishing to establish himself

in business in the vicinity. Their instructions were simple: to remit voluminous reports detailing the gossip about the crime, the movements of the various principals, family histories, and so forth, including sketches, tracings, and measurements. Nothing was too trivial or too remote to be included. The various principals were indiscriminately "shadowed" wherever they went.

When Twain writes to Howells [in January 1879] about *Simon Wheeler, Detective* he says, "I have very extravagantly burlesqued the detective business—if it is possible to burlesque that business extravagantly."

—Virginia S. Hale, "Mark Twain, Detective." *Connecticut Review* 14, no. 1 (Spring 1992): pp. 79–80.

PETER MESSENT ON THE ELEPHANT AS SYMBOLIC OF A HOAX

[Peter Messent's 1997 study of Mark Twain opens with a chapter dedicated to "The Stolen White Elephant," in which the author questions the purpose of using an elephant in the first place as the focus of the action in the tale. In this extract, Messent explains the linguistic connotation that the elephant would have evoked for Twain's contemporary readers; that is, a hoax:]

Any of Twain's contemporaries reading with even one metaphorical eye open would probably have made the connection between the subject of Twain's story and the frontier expression 'seeing the Elephant.' Forrest G. Robinson speaks of Twain's own predisposition during his years in the Far West (described in *Roughing It*) to 'fall lock, stock and barrel for the practical joke that the mining frontier amounted to.' To see the Elephant, in this mining context, was to be aware of this joke, to see through the hoax. For behind western illusions of wealth and success lay mainly 'the Elephant of gross self-deception and inevitable failure.' Robinson comments further on the way Twain's art relates to the hoax that the frontier turned out to be, when he writes that 'having seen the Elephant, [Twain] would plant a whole herd.' In the title and subject matter of this sketch is the clear acknowledgement of one such (individual) literary planting.

When Marcel Gutwirth describes comic surprise in terms of 'the good laugh at [one's] own expense' that follows 'the joyous sense of having been had—in no very material sense, however—and having got over it,' he might have had the hoax in mind. Twain was a master of the deadpan and his earlier famous sketch, 'Jim Smiley and his Jumping Frog', foregrounds the difficulty of penetrating narrative imposture: 'because Simon Wheeler never breaks his own deadpan presentation, we never know exactly who is the duper and who is the duped.' The question of the identity of the hoaxer is also a central one in 'The Stolen White Elephant.' Its main narrator, the aged gentleman, is unflinchingly deadpan throughout the story, but there is little evidence of any hoax being played on his part. His deadpan appears not to conceal anything. It would seem, rather, to be a way of representing both his naivete and gullibility. For the narrative ends with an affirmation of his 'undimmed . . . admiration' for Inspector Blunt as 'the greatest detective the world has ever produced,' despite all the evidence both of the detective's ineptitude and of the narrator's own duping.

—Peter Messent, *Mark Twain* (London: MacMillan Press, 1997): pp. 4–5.

Plot Summary of
"The Man That Corrupted Hadleyburg"

For three generations, Hadleyburg had been known as the most principled town around. Hadleyburg protected its reputation ardently: "It was so proud of it, and so anxious to insure its perpetuation, that it began to teach the principles of honest dealings to its babies in the cradle, and made the like teachings the staple of their culture thenceforward through all the years devoted to their education." There are nineteen principal families in Hadleyburg whose members are particularly revered for their honesty and trustworthiness.

The first part of the story, setting up the circumstances for its eventual fall, explains that other towns were jealous of Hadleyburg and considered its citizens quite vain. But, Hadleyburg was "an incorruptible town," until one day the town had the bad luck of insulting a passing stranger. Whether anyone in Hadleyburg was aware of the offense or not, the stranger remembered it and spent the next year plotting revenge. He thought of many possibilities but finally settled on one plan that would have an effect on the entire town.

Six months later, the stranger showed up in Hadleyburg around 10 p.m. one evening at the home of the cashier of the bank, Mr. Richards. Because the old cashier was not at home, his wife attended the stranger, who told Mrs. Richards that he had been told to leave a sack of money in the care of her husband. He considered his job now complete, he said, and told her that she would never see him again. After the stranger left, Mrs. Richards immediately looked at the note attached to the bag. In the note, she read that the sack contained 160 pounds of gold—roughly $40,000 in their day—which was destined for a kind citizen of Hadleyburg that had befriended an unlucky gambler two years earlier. The only condition for collecting the contents of the bag was that the good Samaritan had to repeat the remark he made to the stranger when he made him a gift of $20. The note also said that Mr. Richards could handle the investigation privately or publicly. If he decided to conduct the search in public then:

> "Thirty days from now, let the candidate appear at the town hall at eight in the evening (Friday), and hand his remark, in a sealed envelope, to the Rev. Mr. Burgess . . . and let Mr. Burgess there and then destroy the seals of the sack, open it, and see if the remark is correct:

> if correct, let the money be delivered, with my sincere gratitude, to my benefactor thus identified."

Mrs. Richards was excited at the thought of so much money and hoped that it was her husband who had befriended the stranger.

When Mr. Richards returned at eleven o'clock, his wife told him of the events. Mr. Richards marveled at both the weight and the value of the bag. He said to his wife: "Why we're rich, Mary, rich; all we've got to do is to bury the money and burn the papers." But Mrs. Richards convinced him otherwise so he left immediately for the shop of Mr. Cox, the printer, to publish the note.

On his return, Mr. Richards and his wife speculated about the identity of the kind citizen. Mrs. Richards was sure that it must have been Barclay Goodson. He had been dead for six months and was the only resident of Hadleyburg who could tell his fellow towns-people how self-righteous they really were. They all hated him for his directness. But then the Richards couple remembered that the town also hated the Reverend Burgess. Mrs. Richards wondered why the stranger had given him the task of handing over the money. It was during this part of their talk that Mr. Richards made a confession to his wife. He had known all along that Burgess was innocent of the transgression that the townspeople had pinned on him. Mr. Richards explained: "I hadn't the pluck to do it. It would have turned everybody against me. I felt mean, ever so mean, but I didn't dare; I hadn't the manliness to face that." Mrs. Richards was more horrified at what Reverend Burgess thought of her husband today than of his lack of honesty in the past.

Because of their talk, Mr. Richards became just as concerned as his wife and he rushed off to stop Mr. Cox from publishing the note. Once at the printer's shop he realized that it was too late, and he and Mr. Cox discuss what would have happened if they had split the wealth. Back at his house, he and his wife agree that all things are ordained and that they must conduct themselves as honest citizens of Hadleyburg. In the meantime, though, one of Mr. Cox's workers notifies the Associated Press about the stranger's note and his reward so that by the next morning Hadleyburg has become national news.

As the word spreads, excitement takes over the whole town. People come to see the sack of gold on display at Pinkerton's bank. The town's nineteen leading families are filled with anticipation because the reputation of Hadleyburg is now sure to spread. All share the opinion that it must have been Goodson who befriended the unknown man, but no one can imagine what he could have said. Three weeks pass and the townspeople's spirits begin to wane. Then Mr. Richards receives a letter signed by Howard L. Stephenson in which the writer divulges that Goodson had befriended the misguided gambler. The letter also disclosed that Goodson told its writer that Richards had done Goodson a favor in the past. So Stephenson concluded that Richards should claim the reward. To do so, he revealed the secret message: "You are far from a bad man: go, and reform." Mrs. Richards was ecstatic at the news, but Richards is disturbed by this since he can't remember ever being of help to Goodson. In the meantime, Stephenson sends the exact same letter to the other eighteen leading families. Once again, spirits are high.

When the day finally arrived, and the stranger's benefactor will be identified, the decorated town hall was filled with the nineteen leading families of Hadleyburg, as well as with people from all over, including news correspondents. After delivering a short speech on the values that Hadleyburg represented, Reverend Burgess opened and read the first letter submitted for the reward. Its author, John Wharton Billson, claims that he assisted the stranger, writing that he told him: "You are very far from being a bad man: go, and reform." Everyone present cheers for Billson. But then Burgess reads the letter sent in by Wilson, a lawyer in town, who makes the same claim, submitting that he said: "You are far from being a bad man: go, and reform." One message contains 'very', the other doesn't. Burgess decides to open the letter contained in the sack of gold. It confirms that Wilson's message is the correct one. A fight between the two men begins, each accusing the other of lying and stealing. Mayhem ensues among the crowd, until Burgess reads the next letter, also written by a member of one of the nineteen leading families of the town. It contains the exact same message as Wilson's. The Reverend continues to open each of the letters he has received; each contains the same message, which the crowd gleefully chants as Burgess reads.

During the ruckus, the Richards become nervous, fearing that like the members of the other eighteen leading families their attempt to gain the stranger's gold fraudulently will be revealed. By luck, however, their letter containing Stephenson's message is not among those read. Instead, Burgess opens the sack and all present discover that the alleged reward of gold is really pieces of gilded lead. The towns-people decide to auction the sack and give the proceeds to Mr. Richards, who has been declared the most honest man in town. A stranger in the crowd bids and wins the bag. He announces that he will engrave the names of the eighteen dishonest families on the false gold pieces, when Harkness, a wealthy manufacturer, convinces the stranger to sell him the lead. Harkness plans to make coins from the lead with the face of his opponent Pinkerton. The stranger declares that Richards deserves a reward for his honesty and gives him three $500 bills as a first deposit.

The Richards couple return home wondering if fate has ordained their unexpected gain. The next day, the stranger brings them checks for $38,500. Mrs. Richards thinks the man is the late-night visitor who left the sack of gold in the first place. Mr. Richards believes that he must be Stephenson. Then Burgess sends Richards a note explaining that he didn't open Richards' letter in public, thus gaining for him the nomination as the most honest, because Richards had helped him once when the town accused him falsely. Richards and his wife, confused by all these accolades, only wish they deserved this good fortune. Soon, their consciences begin to plague them. They become mortally sick with worry and, in their delirium, confess the truth about their dishonesty and the innocence of Burgess. This spoils for good Hadleyburg's once unblemished reputation. The legislature then passes a new law to remove the word '*not*' from the town motto so that it now reads: "Lead Us into Temptation." ❀

List of Characters in
"The Man That Corrupted Hadleyburg"

Edward Richards: A stranger leaves a sealed bag allegedly containing gold as a reward to the citizen of Hadleyburg who once was kind to the stranger with Richards, the bank clerk. Richards is tempted by the gold. Although Richards is believed to be the most honest citizen in Hadleyburg, he is later found to be a fraud.

Mrs. Richards: She regularly reminds her husband, either by chiding him or by her nervous state, that he should continue to behave honestly; however, she goes along with Richards' scheme to acquire the Stranger's gold. Both Mrs. Richards and her husband suffer an unpleasant end because of their dishonesty.

Reverend Burgess: According to the directions in the stranger's note, the benefactor must deliver a sealed letter to the Reverend containing the words said to the stranger in order to collect the reward. Burgess has been rejected by the townspeople because of a past offense; Mr. Richards is the only person in town who knows that Burgess is really innocent.

Cox, the newspaperman: Cox publishes the note given to Richards by the stranger seeking the man who befriended him. Because of this, Hadleyburg, and its reputation for being incorruptible, becomes national news.

Barclay Goodson: Recently deceased, Goodson was hated by the community because he publicly questioned their self-righteous behavior. Most people in town believe that Goodson was probably the man that the stranger sought.

Howard L. Stephenson: This is the writer of a letter that Richards receives after the news has spread of the impending reward. According to the letter, Stephenson saw Goodson give $20 to a stranger. The letter also reveals the message that is needed to collect the reward: "You are far from being a bad man; go, and reform."

Billson and *Wilson:* Two of the first citizens to have their messages read in public. Both claim to be the stranger's benefactor. Wilson temporarily gains the public's support until Reverend Burgess opens the other sealed envelopes, all containing the same message.

Dr. Harkness: Harkness buys the bag of gilded lead from the stranger and then makes coins from the lead with the face of Pinkerton, his opponent in the race for the state legislature.

Critical Views on
"The Man That Corrupted Hadleyburg"

EARL F. BRIDEN AND MARY PRESCOTT
ON MR. AND MRS. RICHARDS

[Both Earl Briden and Mary Prescott are professors of
English at Bryant College. Briden's articles have appeared
in *Studies in Short Fiction*, the *Shaw Review*, and *American
Notes and Queries*, while Prescott's area of interest is the
modern and contemporary novel. In this extract, the authors
consider the characters of Mr. and Mrs. Richards:]

In the experience of his central characters, then, Twain brings
together two apparently contradictory ideas. Like their fellow towns-
people, old Edward and Mary Richards are motivated by two forms
of self-contentment. In the past they acted on the sentimental
imperative, conforming to the principles of honesty in which they
were trained and thus, by gaining approval of a God-like public
opinion, gaining self-approval. The diabolical stranger activates in
them the second primary means of self-gratification, the pocket-
book imperative in which, Twain implies, they have also been
trained. On the one hand, then, they and their neighbors are selfish.
On the other hand, this selfishness manifests itself in behavior that is
machine-like—repetitive, automatic, duplicated by citizen after citizen—and attests to the uniformity of the Master Passion in Hadleyburg. And, Twain says in *What Is Man?*, this Ruler is all that the
individual can find when he seeks his ego, his self, his identity, when,
in psychological terms, he seeks to become an object to himself.
Twain's spokesman points out that people like to imagine a definite,
autonomous "I" presiding over their faculties; but, he continues,
"when we try to define him we find we cannot do it." The only
master of man-the-machine is a capricious, absolute conscience that
seeks its own contentment, a ruler whose form is both determining
and, as its uniformity in Hadleyburg helps to suggest, determined.

One potential objection to the view that "Hadleyburg" is a syn-
thesis, in popular fictional form, of these ideas is that Twain singled
out the Richardses for a fate ultimately different from their neighbors' and thus seems to be invoking the microscopic self of his work

of the 1880s. Here it should be recalled that in *The Mysterious Stranger* and his 1910 essay, "The Turning Point of My Life," Twain buttressed his psychological theories with a second determinist scheme, arguing that life's course consists of a chain of linked events, each determining the next and determined, in turn, by its predecessor. This article will suggest that, in tracing the old couple's divergence from the collective behavior of their peers, Twain was dramatizing this complementary view of mechanistic determinism. The destiny of his central characters, in short, is doubly fixed—partly by their participation in the collective identity, partly by the compulsion of their life-chains, whose fateful turning points are symbolized, ironically, by their would-be benefactor, Reverend Burgess.

> —Earl F. Briden and Mary Prescott, "The Lie that I am I: Paradoxes of Identity in Mark Twain's 'Hadleyburg.'" *Studies in Short Fiction* 21, no. 4 (Fall 1984): pp. 385–86.

☙

SUSAN K. HARRIS ON SOURCES FOR THE STORY

> [In this extract, Susan Harris, a professor at Queens College, provides a possible historical link for the theme and characters in the Hadleyburg story. Professor Harris cites the *Missionary Herald,* a Congregational Church periodical, and the Asylum Hill Congregational Church in Hartford, Connecticut, as probable sources for the tale:]

In fact, the specific audience Twain may have had in mind is signaled by the MISSIONARY HERALD Mary Richards is reading as the stranger enters her house. Established in 1805, the MISSIONARY HERALD was a Congregational Church periodical that enjoyed immense popularity throughout the nineteenth century and well into the middle of the twentieth. Largely consisting of journal reports from missionaries abroad, it provided stay-at-homes with vicarious thrills concerning the perils of the faith in alien climes. Certainly one reason for its inclusion in "Hadleyburg" was to provide a touch of local color; another was to provide ironic comment on Mrs. Richards' own lack of spiritual grace. As one of Twain's (always satiric) "practicing Christians," she feels more concern for the pagans abroad than for her own soul. But the name of the magazine also identifies Twain's target audience, people who read the MISSIONARY HERALD as well as literary journals—that is, literary (and usually wealthy) members of the Congregational Church. Part of the liberal Protestant Establishment, the MISSIONARY HERALD's sponsors included not only congregations like Henry Ward Beecher's Plymouth Church (whose members Twain had satirized in THE INNOCENTS ABROAD thirty years earlier) but also Hartford's Asylum Hill Congregational Church, where Twain's best friend, the Reverend Joseph Twichell, had occupied the pulpit since 1865.

The congregations from Brooklyn Heights and Asylum Hill fit the profile of the ideal readers for "Hadleyburg" exactly: grandchildren of Americans of a sterner faith, they were educated, affluent, and occasionally concerned about the effect of their money on their souls. In 1869 Twain had written Livy that he had "reread Beecher's sermon on the love of riches being the root of evil," an indication that Beecher, at least in the early days of Twain's association with the wealthy Congregationalist crowd, was trying to instill some sense of moral conscience into his parishioners, but as Twain's portrayal of Beecher's "Pilgrims" in INNOCENTS suggests, even then their consciences were of the verbal rather than the active breed. As the years passed, ministers like Beecher (in whom Twain lost faith after the minister's affair with Mrs. Tilton was exposed) and Twichell more often helped their congregations rationalize their money-lust than attacked them for it. Equally important, whatever attack they did mount was framed by the evolution of a liberal version of the doctrine of free will—or, from the opposite point of view, by the degeneration of the doctrine of predestination. Overseen by the spirit of reformers like Horace Bushnell, the Arminian strain of Congregationalist theology had come to the fore, emphasizing man's natural capacity for enlightened reform and de-emphasizing the concept of original sin. Like the sentimental fiction which implied that all problems could be resolved by those willing to confront their difficulties and work hard to untangle them, the messages such ministers gave their people held that no sinner who truly wanted to change was incorrigible—a message so familiar that, in "Hadleyburg," when the Stranger claims it to have been Goodson's words to him, not one member of the community doubts that the misanthrope would have said it.

—Susan K. Harris, "'Hadleyburg': Mark Twain's Dual Attack on Banal Theology and Banal Literature." *American Literary Realism* 16, no. 2 (Autumn 1983): pp. 246–47.

MARY E. RUCKER ON THE RICHARDS' REDEMPTION

[A scholar who has written on both Nathaniel Hawthorne and Mark Twain, Mary Rucker maintains that the driving force for the citizens' actions in "Hadleyburg" is money lust. Because of this, they ignore their moral principles. In this excerpt, Rucker focuses on the moral dilemma that the Richards represent, and questions whether it is redemption or delirium that provokes their final confession:]

From this point to the end of their crisis, the Richardses are victims of a fear that leads to distorted perceptions. It compels them to see the customary sermon as an accusatory sermon "aimed straight and specially at the people who were concealing deadly sins." Further, it leads them to believe that Burgess, aware of Edward's refusal to clear him of imputed guilt, deliberately ignores their oeillade. Edward's rashly convincing himself that his maid overheard his telling Mary of his failing Burgess attests to the intensity of his fear and the extent to which it overpowers his reason. When he questions Sarah, his own hysterical guilt leads Edward to interpret her frustration as evidence of her guilt. "When they were alone again," we are told, Mary and Edward "began to piece many unrelated things together and get horrible results out of the combination." The most awful issue of their frenzied thought is the conviction that Burgess's note is sarcastic and that the wronged minister retains Edward's letter as a trap. They are finally convinced that he has exposed them.

Certainly the couple's drives—fear and delirium—qualify the contention that the Richardses' death-bed confession signifies a moral regeneration. The matrix of the opportunities they have had to act morally is such that Mary and Edward must act willfully. The inadvertent death-bed revelations of guilt are obviously not willed but rather delirious acts. Nor is the destruction of the checks willed. True, Edward comes to see them in moral terms: "'They came from Satan. I saw the hell-brand on them, and I knew they were sent to betray me to sin.'" Yet, he burns them primarily because of the driving fear of eternally damning his soul. Both the destruction of the checks and the Richardses' unintended revelation of their guilt are, then, compulsive rather than rationally willed acts and hence are morally neutral.

Just as worthless in terms of the implied ethics of the story is the confession that Edward makes in one of his lucid moments. Although that confession is valid insofar as he courageously acknowledges both his betrayal of Burgess and his attempt to steal, its amoral if not impure motive—the erroneous convictions that Sarah has publicized his failing Burgess and that Burgess, in revenge, has exposed him—undermine its value. Edward, after all, merely acknowledges what he believes to be public, and nothing suggests that he would have chosen to make the acknowledgment otherwise. Further, the object of his admitting his culpability is "manhood," not moral rectitude in and for itself: he believes that he will die a "man" and not a dog cowered by shame if he assents to the supposedly revealed facts. The misdirected self-righteousness with which he magnanimously "forgives" Burgess, to whom he turned a deaf ear when the innocent minister attempted to inform him of his error, also undermines the confession. To the very end, the Richardses fail to act consciously and deliberately for primarily moral ends.

—Mary E. Rucker, "Moralism and Determination in 'The Man that Corrupted Hadlyburg.'" *Studies in Short Fiction* 14, no. 1 (Winter 1977): pp. 53–54.

⊛

GARY SCHARNHORST ON THE STRANGER

[Gary Scharnhorst, a professor at the University of Texas at Dallas, is the author of *Horatio Alger, Jr.* (1980) and articles on James, Emerson, and Twain. In this essay, Scharnhorst compares Twain's "Hadleyburg" with Milton's *Paradise Lost*, discussing the stranger figure as a Satan seeking revenge, in the context of Milton's Arch-Fiend:]

By his own admission, Twain was intrigued by the literary and theological *élan* of Milton's epic. As early as 1858, he wrote his brother Orion that he considered "the grandest thing" in it to be "the Arch-Fiend's terrible energy!" He wrote Olivia Langdon in 1869 that after their marriage they would enjoy together "the drum-beats of Milton's stately sentences." In 1877, however, he listed *Paradise Lost* among those works he would have burned had they been submitted to him for publication, and two years later he whimsically claimed in a letter to Howells that Orion had planned "to write a burlesque" of the epic. Twain apparently had come to regret that Milton consigned the Prince of Darkness to an ignominious end—"I have always felt friendly toward Satan," as he declared in his Autobiography—so, in 1898, he expressed an intention to rehabilitate Satan's reputation and completed "The Man That Corrupted Hadleyburg" in which he initially undertook that project by revising Miton's version of the Fall. Certainly, Twain was influenced by *Paradise Lost* in several other late works, for he modeled parts of *A Connecticut Yankee* (1889), "Extracts from Adam's Diary" (1893), and *The Mysterious Stranger* (composed 1898–1906) on the epic, and he proclaimed in 1900 that it was "a work that everybody wants to have read and nobody wants to read."

The parallels between *Paradise Lost* and "Hadleyburg Corrupted" may be most easily discerned by comparing incidents in Twain's story with analogues in Milton's epic. In the story, a "revengeful" stranger resolves to "invent a compensating satisfaction" for a vague offense suffered in the town and "contrives many plans, and all of them were good, but none of them was quite sweeping enough." This stranger wants "a plan which would comprehend the entire town, and not let so much as one person escape unhurt. At last he had a fortunate idea, and when it fell into his brain it lit up his whole head with an evil joy. He began to form a plan at once, saying to himself, 'That is the thing to do—I will corrupt the town.'" His fortunately-fallen resolution parallels that of Milton's Arch-Fiend who, "Stirred up with envy and revenge," decides to retaliate for his dismissal from Heaven and considers a variety of plans in demonic council. Like Twain's stranger, this Satan disdains common revenge.

He wishes "to confound the race Of mankind in one root," and when Beelzebub details his "bold design" to the other fallen angels assembled in Pandemonium "joy Sparkled in all their eyes." Twain's satanic stranger then travels to Hadleyburg where he delivers a bag presumably filled with gold coins to Mary Richards, who "gently quivering with excitement" succumbs to coveting the wealth. Similarly, Milton's Satan, after his epic voyage to earth, excites "the organ of [Eve's] fancy" by whispering to her as she sleeps. Just as Mary welcomes home her husband by declaring she is "'so glad you've come," Eve wakes to greet Adam the next morning by declaring, "'glad I see Thy face.'" In contrast, none of these details appears in Genesis 3.

—Gary Scharnhorst, "Paradise Revisited: Twain's 'The Man that Corrupted Hadlyburg.'" *Studies in Short Fiction* 18, no. 1 (Winter 1981): pp. 60–61.

⊗

HOWARD G. BAETZHOLD ON THE INFLUENCE OF WILLIAM LECKY

[In his 1970 work *Mark Twain and John Bull*, Howard G. Baetzhold analyzed the effects of William Edward Hartpole Lecky's *History of European Morals from Augustus to Charlemagne* (1869) on Mark Twain's writings. In this extract, Baetzhold explains the relationship he sees between Twain's "Hadleyburg" and his apparent interest in the moral concepts expressed by the English philosopher Lecky:]

The most successful fictional expression of the principles set forth in the humorist's "Bible" is the bitter short story, "The Man that Corrupted Hadleyburg." Written in Austria between August and October, 1898, almost immediately after the first draft of *What is Man?*, the tale effectively projects the author's withering scorn for man's pretensions. Yet it, too, concludes on a somewhat positive note.

Reading this story as an additional phase of the "discussion with Lecky" is further justified by the fact that Clemens took the text for his sardonic sermon from that same encyclopedic first chapter of

European Morals. As far as its central point is concerned, the author was agreeing with Lecky, for the passage in question points out the absurdity of the theological notion that one must avoid any sin, however trivial. As the historian puts it, such a tenet would require the suppression of all desires, the avoiding of all temptations. One would have to ignore the fact that temptations can serve to elevate moral character and that "a torpid sinlessness is not a high moral condition." Hence, such a notion is not only absurd, but could actually serve to "paralyze our moral being."

In the story, the "moral being" of the Hadleyburgers is indeed paralyzed. Proud of their town's reputation for incorruptibility, they had trained their children in "principles of honesty" from the cradle onward. To allow that honesty to "solidify," they removed all temptations from the experiences of their young people. Secure in their own convictions, with "Lead Us Not Into Temptation" as their town's motto, they remained totally unaware that this "torpid sinlessness" was actually corrupt.

When temptation finally does appear in the form of an alleged fortune in gold coins, greed rapidly supplants the heretofore untested honesty, and the town's demise is swift. Paradoxically (and just as Lecky indicates), the temptation to sin later results in the beginnings of a "moral elevation" for Hadleyburg. Even more ironically, the very temptation itself originates in a sin—a desire for revenge harbored by the "passing stranger" whom the town had chanced to offend some years earlier. Though acting from an evil motive in devising the fraud that tempts all the "best" people of Hadleyburg, he actually becomes an agent of good in opening the villagers' eyes to the absurdity of their pious pretensions.

> —Howard G. Baetzhold, *Mark Twain and John Bull* (Bloomington, Ind.: Indiana University Press, 1970): pp. 226–27.

✺

PHILIP S. FONER ON ARTIFICIAL HONESTY IN THE STORY

[Philip S. Foner edited collections of writings by Abraham Lincoln, George Washington, and Thomas Jefferson, and his books include *Mark Twain: Social Critic, Jack London: American Rebel, History of the Labor Movement in the United States,* and *Jews in American History.* In this excerpt, Foner discusses what Twain considered the "artificial honesty" of the Hadleyburg townspeople. Foner quotes on religion and hypocrisy from Mark Twain's notebook to further elucidate the idea of moral and religious artificiality:]

The *artificial honesty* is illustrated in the successful efforts of the villagers to salvage their consciences. One very religious couple who permitted an innocent man, whom they might have saved, to be indicted, are relieved of any sense of shame or feeling of guilt when they learn that he does not suspect their betrayal. The wife exclaims: "Oh . . . I am glad of that! As long as he doesn't know that you could have saved him, he—he—well, that makes it a great deal better."

Throughout the tale Twain mocks an artificial, untried piety, and advocates omitting the negative in the line of the Lord's Prayer: "Lead us not into temptation." He urges the pious, smug moralist, with their shallow, hypocritical rectitude, "to request that they be led into temptation, rather than away from it, in order that they might make their moral fibre strong enough through use instead of rotten through inactivity." He was thus reaffirming the creed of John Milton, who had written almost three hundred years before: "I cannot praise a fugitive and cloistered virtue unexercised and unbreathed, that never sallies out and seeks her adversary but slinks out of the race, where the immortal garland is to be run for, not without dust and heat."

In an unpublished comment in his notebook, set down about the time he was writing "The Man That Corrupted Hadleyburg," Twain indicated the chief lesson of the story: "The Land of Cant. That is always a land where the great bulk of the people are sincerely religious." Sincerity in religion was not enough; it nurtured hypocrites, not truly religious people. What was needed was a religion which would create people willing to act in public life on the religious principles they professed in private life. "There are Christian Private Morals," Twain noted, "but there are not Christian Public Morals." He called upon all citizens "to throw away their public morals and use none but their private ones henceforth in all their activities."

—Philip S. Foner, *Mark Twain Social Critic* (New York: International Publishers, 1958): pp. 141–42. ☺

Plot Summary of
"The £1,000,000 Note"

When a weekend sailing excursion in the San Francisco bay goes wrong, the narrator of this story, a young man named Henry Adams, finds himself stranded in open waters. Eventually, a ship bound for London rescues him, and he works to pay for his passage until the ship docks in London. At the end of the journey, the narrator disembarks in the unfamiliar city, tired and shabby, with only a dollar in his pocket. This money buys him food and lodging for one day only. During the next 24 hours, he goes hungry as he walks aimlessly about London. On seeing a child throw away an uneaten pear, the narrator makes several attempts to pick it up but is too embarrassed. Out of nowhere, he hears a voice inviting him inside a nearby home.

As the narrator later discovers, the two occupants of the house are elderly gentlemen brothers who had been discussing for some time what would happen if an intelligent and honest man were given a £1,000,000 note. They decided that the only way to settle their argument would be to agree to a bet. Brother A bet that such a man, left alone in a city with no friends, would starve. Brother B believed that he would not. The brothers spent several days observing passersby to find just the right man. Noticing the narrator's struggle with his pride over picking up the dropped pear, the brothers decided that he fit their qualifications: an honest, well-bred man who was down on his luck.

When Adams entered the house, the two gentlemen did not explain their bet. Instead, they gave the narrator an envelope, asked him to consider the enclosed proposition carefully, and then said good-bye to him. On leaving, the narrator was understandably upset because they had not invited him to share their unfinished breakfast and the discarded pear had now disappeared.

However, when the narrator opened the contents of the envelope, his spirits changed immediately. He found money and a note. Forgetting all else, the narrator went directly to the first inn he could find. He ate well and happily, but when he took out the money to pay his bill, he noticed that the owner of the inn stared at him in a very peculiar way. Adams realized that he held a bill worth

£1,000,000—worth, in his day, five million dollars! Thinking quickly, Adams told the inn's proprietor that the £1,000,000 note was the smallest bill he had, and asked for change. The owner, obviously impressed by such an amount of money, told him that he could settle his bill some other time and suggested that the narrator put the note out of sight.

Back on the street, the narrator thought that the two gentlemen had made a terrible mistake. When he returned to their house, their servant told him that the men had left for a trip and would not return for a month. It was then that the narrator remembered that a letter had been in the envelope the brothers gave him. The letter said:

> "You are an intelligent and honest man, as one may see by your face. We conceive you to be poor and a stranger. Enclosed you will find a sum of money. It is lent to you for thirty days, without interest. Report at this house at the end of that time. I have a bet on you. If I win it you shall have any situation that is in my gift—any, that is, that you shall be able to prove yourself familiar with and competent to fill."

The narrator, confused and puzzled, spent some time reflecting on all the possibilities. His conclusions were that since he didn't know the reason for the loan, he shouldn't worry about that. He concentrated, instead, on the prospect of having work and a salary in thirty days.

With this thought, the fellow began to feel much better. As he walked, he passed a tailor's shop and decided that he wanted to discard his shabby old clothes for new ones. He hesitated many times because he didn't have any money other than the £1,000,000 note. Finally, he entered the shop. The attendant ignored him for a while, and then showed the man the worst clothes in the store. Because they were better than the ones he was wearing, the narrator decided to purchase them, so he asked the clerk if he could pay him over time for the clothes. The attendant made an unpleasant remark and treated the man impolitely. When the narrator explained that he didn't have any small change, the attendant's attitude became even less civil—until the man handed over the £1,000,000 note. The reaction on the clerk's face and in his attitude was both immediate and obvious. When the proprietor of the store asked what was going on, the clerk showed him the note. At that point, the shop owner took over and began to treat the narrator as a rich gentleman. He took Adams' measurements and started giving orders to his assistants for all sorts of fine clothes. When the narrator protested and explained that he could only pay over time, the proprietor gladly agreed to any condition of payment. The confused narrator left the store slowly realizing that by showing, and never cashing, the £1,000,000 note, he could buy whatever he wanted.

In a week's time, the narrator had completely changed his circumstances. He returned to the inn where his luck had started. Because of the narrator's new-found fame, the innkeeper's business had increased remarkably, for his hotel was the place where the "vest-pocket million-pounder" lived. News of the narrator's activities surfaced in the newspapers with increasing coverage daily; his caricature even appeared in the magazine *Punch*. Just for fun, the narrator kept his old shabby clothes and wore them at times to provoke mistreatment from shopowners before pulling out the £1,000,000 note, but soon even this was impossible because he was so easily recognized.

After ten days, Adams paid his respects to the American ambassador in London. He was received very cordially and invited to stay for dinner. As it turned out, the ambassador had been friends with the narrator's father, and they had attended Yale together; as a result, the ambassador issued an open invitation for the narrator to spend as much of his free time with him as desired. The narrator considered it wise to accept such a generous offer, thinking ahead to what would happen at the end of his 30-day spree. He had been carefully keeping his expenditures to within what he thought he could pay from the salary promised by the brothers who had loaned him the note, but he couldn't be absolutely sure that he would not be ruined financially.

At the dinner that evening, the narrator found himself one of fourteen guests. Most were titled English nobility, but among the visitors that evening was a young English girl named Portia Langham, with whom Adams fell in love immediately. Another guest, Lloyd Hastings, turned out to be an acquaintance of the narrator. This meeting was a great surprise for both men, and they reminisced about the good old days. When Hastings asked how Adams had come into his fortune, Adams promised to tell him at the end of the 30-day period. In the meantime, though, Adams and Hastings discussed business activities, and the narrator spent the rest of a delightful evening getting to know the lovely Portia.

Not only did Adams declare his love to Portia that night, he also blurted out the entire story of the £1,000,000 note. Unexpectedly, Portia laughed at the details of his tale, which caused considerable confusion in Adams: "What in the nation she could find to laugh about, I couldn't see but there it was; every half minute some new detail would fetch her, and I would have to stop as much as a minute and a half to give her a chance to settle down again." But her reaction made Adams love her all the more. That evening they decided to marry, but Adams insisted that they would have to wait a few years until he earned a good salary and caught up on his debts. He also asked Portia to accompany him to the brothers' residence on the thirtieth day. Portia agreed, continued to tease him because she said that she did not believe his story.

After the dinner, Hastings and Adams walked home together. During their stroll, Hastings did all the talking—about his invest-ment ventures—while Adams could only think of Portia. When they arrived at Adams' rooms, Hastings marveled at the luxurious accom-modations, which provoked renewed anxieties in Adams: "Deep in debt, not a cent in the world, a lovely girl's happiness or woe in my hands, and nothing in front of me but a salary which might never— oh, would never—materialize! Oh, oh, oh, I am ruined past hope; nothing can save me!" Then Adams admitted to Hastings that he hadn't heard a word his friend had said, because he was so lost in thought about Portia and their plans to marry. Hastings congratu-lated him heartily and then proceeded patiently to tell Adams again the full story of his investment scheme. Hastings wanted to sell shares in a mining project, but had been unable to find any buyers. He was very concerned because time was running out on his option, and he would soon lose the money he had invested, so he asked Adams to give him money for the venture. Instead, Adams devised a plan where Hastings would use his name as the major investment creditor and they would share whatever profits materialized.

This ingenious plan became news all over London the next after-noon. Over the next few days, Adams stayed at home and to all inquiries recommended Hastings and his mining project. In the evenings, he went to the ambassador's home to visit with Portia and to talk of their love and his expectations for the promised salary.

At the end of the 30 days, thanks to their successful mining investment, Adams and Hastings each had a million dollars in the bank. Adams met Portia at the ambassador's home. As they walked, Adams felt so good that mentally he raised his own salary. At the old gentlemen's house, the servant welcomed the two and ushered them in to see Brother A and Brother B. Adams introduced Portia to them as his future wife. He returned the £1,000,000 note to the delight of the winning brother, who could now collect his £20,000 bet. Then Adams notified them of the £200,000 profit he had made by the use of the borrowed note. Portia, who did not know about the successful venture with Hastings, was happily surprised at the news of Adams' profit. When the brothers offered Adams his promised job, he politely declines, saying that they do not have a position that he wants. When, however, Portia reveals that one of the brothers is actually her stepfather, Adams does ask for a job—that of son-in-law. They marry, live happily ever after, and keep the cancelled £1,000,000 note as a framed memento of their good fortune. ❀

List of Characters in
"The £1,000,000 Note"

Henry Adams: The narrator of this story, Adams is down on his luck in an unfamiliar city, London, when he is unexpectedly given a £1,000,000 note to use as he likes for thirty days. No one he meets is able to make change for the large bill; instead, all offer him credit, and soon Adams finds himself rich and very famous.

Brother A and *Brother B:* Two elderly English gentlemen who make a wager on whether a man can survive for a month with only a £1,000,000 bank note. Brother A believes that the man given the money will not survive the month, while Brother B bets that the man receiving the unusual gift will do well.

Portia Langham: At a dinner at the American ambassador's house, the 22-year-old English woman meets Adams and they fall in love. She tells Adams that she doesn't believe his story about the £1,000,000 bank note, but accompanies him on the thirtieth day to the brothers' home. As it turns out, Brother B, the winner of the wager, is her stepfather. Portia and Henry Adams marry at the end of the tale, keeping the cancelled bank note as a souvenir.

Lloyd Hastings: A friend of Henry Adams from America, Hastings is failing in his investment project until Adams begins telling others about his plan. As a result, Hastings is able to sell his mining stock, and each earn $200,000 in profit. ❈

Critical Views on
"The £1,000,000 Note"

PHILIP S. FONER ON MONEY LUST

[Philip S. Foner edited collections of writings by Abraham Lincoln, George Washington, and Thomas Jefferson, and his books include *Mark Twain: Social Critic, Jack London: American Rebel, History of the Labor Movement in the United States,* and *Jews in American History.* In this excerpt, he discusses several of Twain's works where the theme of money lust appears. According to Foner, in "The £100,000 Note" Twain demonstrates that all too often a man's standing in society is dependent on his possession of wealth:]

The doctrine of wealth set forth in the "Open Letter to Com. Vanderbilt" was to appear again and again in Twain's writing. It was expressed, as we have already seen, in "The Revised Catechism," in "The Letter From the Recording Angel," *The Gilded Age,* and "The Man that Corrupted Hadleyburg." We also find it in a fragment about a man who went mad through "money-lust," imagined that there was thirty centuries' interest due him, "and he kept calculating & compounding it & laying before lawyers to help him collect it or tell him where to apply. He is *always* calculating it & worrying over it." We find it, too, in a little story about an Esquimau maiden whose life was ruined when her father became rich. Tracing the deterioration of the girl's father, Twain depicts how wealth hardens a man's heart and coarsens his character. He shows how the opinions of the rich man were enhanced by his money in the eyes of society, although they were the same stupid ideas formerly ignored by the same society. "He has lowered the tone of all our tribe," the daughter tells the narrator. "Once they were a frank and manly race, now they are measly hypocrites, and sodden with servility. In my heart of hearts I hate all the ways of millionaires."

Twain's celebrated short story, "The Million Pound Bank Note," recently made into a delightful film by the British moviemaker Ronald Neame, presents his acid comments on a society that treats people according to how much money they have. The tale revolves about a bet between two immensely rich old Londoners over

whether the simple possession of a million pound note would be
enough to insure the future of the man who held it, even if he never
cashed it. To resolve the argument they turn the bill over to an
impoverished American passer-by, with the instructions to return it
in a month's time and claim his reward. At once a despised tramp is
changed into the object of respect and veneration. And the irony of
it all is that it is the appearance of money and not the money itself
that really counts. As long as the American has his scrap of paper, his
credit is unlimited. The finest restaurants, tailors, and hotels—even
the finest homes—are open to him. An occasional flash of the note is
sufficient to establish his credit. He can make stocks rise at the mere
mention of his interest in them. And, of course, he promptly
becomes England's most eligible bachelor.

Twain's farcial story brilliantly satirizes a system based not so
much on money as the appearance of money. Again Twain makes
the point that it is not character but possession of wealth that deter-
mines a man's standing in this contemporary society.

> —Philip S. Foner, *Mark Twain Social Critic* (New York: International
> Publishers, 1958): pp. 159–60.

⊛

MAXWELL GEISMAR ON HISTORICAL CONTEXT OF "THE £1,000,000 NOTE"

[Maxwell Geismar's books include *Writers in Crisis: The
American Novel, 1925–1940, Henry James and the Jacobites,*
and *Mark Twain: An American Prophet.* He has also edited
collections of short stories by Ring Lardner, Thomas Wolfe,
and Jack London. In this extract, Professor Geismar places
"The £1,000,000 Note" in historical context, describing the
financial atmosphere of Clemens' day:]

"The One Hundred Thousand Pound Bank-Note," published in
1893 and also inserted in a later edition of *Merry Tales,* was a trick
tale of a young American who was given a fabulous sum of money as
part of a betting proposition between two British financiers. It is

another ironic parable of unexpected (and undeserved) wealth; and it is interesting to notice how many other stories by Mark Twain in the early nineties dealt with various aspects of this theme. The get-rich-quick mania was the central folk myth of the period; and wasn't Samuel Clemens himself an example of this historical American dream—or nightmare? This was the period of boom and depression in steady succession; of financial wizardry and fiscal legerdemain; of the great Wall Street battles for control, power and manipulation of the new corporations, combines, and monopolies. It was the period of our "interior colonization," so to speak—the development of the internal American empire which, having devoured the enormous wealth of one continent, would soon stretch out its claws for tempting foreign treats. The dominance of this new tribe of cunning, ruthless, unscrupulous, and amoral financial titans and tycoons would change the whole nature of American life as Sam Clemens had known it. In another sense his work may be interpreted as half a lyrical recall of the past, and half an angry, bitter, savage attack on contemporary American society and what he called the future "monarchy" or dictatorship.

But meanwhile he too had shared all the comforts and luxury and material conveniences of sudden wealth on his part, inherited wealth on Livy's part, and now he was suddenly about to taste all the ignoble, sordid, and harrowing consequences of the reverse side— the sudden bankruptcies in this gaudy epoch of primitive finance capitalism—of this negative proposition of the late nineteenth-century American historical scene. At the peak of his own private Gilded Age, Clemens had filled the Hartford mansion with illustrious guests from all over the world. Deserting the Republican party on principle, as a Mugwump, he was intimate with President Cleveland. He associated with such celebrities as Augustin Daly, Edwin Booth, John Drew, the dramatic critic Brander Matthews, and the architect Stanford White. He knew Andrew Carnegie, Jay Gould, Thomas Edison, Whitelaw Reid of the New York *Tribune*, and the Comstock millionaire John Mackay who was just then trying to break the Goulds' monopoly in Western Union. Most of these figures would be described in Clemens' later essays on the American ruling class, or in his *Autobiography*; these reflections form a remarkable chapter in American literature.

—Maxwell Geismar, *Mark Twain: An American Prophet* (Boston: Houghton Mifflin Company, 1970): pp. 130–32. ☯

[In this extract, James L. Johnson postulates that the dark moral struggle so often visible in the works of Twain and Emerson may be linked to the loss of a child by both in the later years of their life, and describes Emerson's struggle to remain flexible as life's experiences jeopardize his investment in idealism:]

Now, in the waning years of his life, Twain was faced a final time with the same desperate disparity that so plagued Emerson. Even one of the precipitous occasions was the same: the death of a child. For Twain, Susy's death transformed the green world to a wasteland, and it was never more terrifyingly real. For Emerson, the death of his son brought about a similar revelation: "This ineffable life which is at my heart will not . . . enter into the details of my biography," he wrote in 1842, "and say to me . . . why my son dies in the sixth year of his joy." "If . . . the world is not a dualism, is not a bipolar Unity, but is *two*, is Me and It, then there is the Alien, the Unknown, and all we have believed & chanted out of our deep instinctive hope is a pretty dream."

For Emerson, the necessary thing was to maintain faith in a vital connection between the Me and the It. Experience—harsh, uncompromising, sharp—had to bend, had to give way to his overwhelming investment in idealism. Whicher points out that as Emerson became more "aware" of experience—of the limitations of human nature—he fell into a provisional skepticism. "He substitutes an ethics of balance," Whicher says, "an Aristotelian quest of the mean, for the suicidal greatness-or-nothing ethics of transcendentalism: 'I know that human strength is not in extremes . . . What is the use of pretending to powers we have not? . . . Why exaggerate the power of virtue? Why be an angel before your time?'"

Yet Emerson could not rest with skepticism. If skepticism "speaks for his deepening respect for experience, his sharpened awareness of the actual frailty and insignificance of man," Emerson nevertheless "springs back to his idealism. If the old confidence in the Deity within was contradicted by the facts, it became that much more intransigent—moved, in short, that much closer to a plain solipsism." In "Experience" Emerson switches quickly from humility to egoism. "Nature, art, persons, letters, religion, objects, successively tumble in, and God is but one of [our] ideas. Nature and literature are subjective phenomena; every evil and every good thing is a shadow from a faith that insulates him from an alien experience, through an uneasy encounter with a monstrous "It," and back to the refuge of a yet more extreme faith.

That Emerson's proud assertion of victory over experience, his claim that "the individual is the world," should be echoed some five decades later by a character named "Satan" is one of the ironies of American literature. Yet that it should be so is not wholly unexpected. Beneath the patina of virtue with which Emerson cloaked his hero there had always stirred something unholy.

—James L. Johnson, *Mark Twain and the Limits of Power: Emerson's God in Ruins* (Knoxville: University of Tennessee Press, 1982): pp. 166–67.

HAROLD H. KOLB JR. ON A COMPARISON OF TWAIN'S EARLY AND LATER WRITINGS

[In this extract, Harold Kolb summarizes the shift in tone that takes place from Twain's early humorous works to the later darker writings, focusing on Twain's unique and sometimes impertinent expression of humor as the key to understanding this shift:]

Mark Twain's early humorous works explode in many directions, with, as Bret Harte noted, "very little moral or aesthetic limitation." Readers who know only *Tom Sawyer* and *Adventures of Huckleberry Finn* would be embarrassed and perhaps shocked by the jokes at the expense of Blacks, Chinese, Jews, Irish, and Indians that occur throughout the apprentice writings. But by 1874 Mark Twain, established as "a scribbler of books, and an immovable fixture among the other rocks of New England," had disciplined his humor and deepened his ideas. Married, settled, celebrated, and turning forty, Twain was proud to be writing for the readers of the *Atlantic Monthly*—"for *it* is the only audience that I sit down before in perfect serenity (for the simple reason that it don't require a 'humorist' to paint himself striped & stand on his head every fifteen minutes.)" In the following fifteen years, Twain produced a succession of major works, from "Old Times on the Mississippi" to *Connecticut Yankee*, that weave together an extraordinary blend of compelling narrative, humorous observation, and perceptive understanding of the human condition. The pure fun of the early pieces has become, as Moncure Conway put it, "fun and . . . philosophy."

In the late works another shift takes place, and though the fun is never entirely lost—the darkest works are illuminated too frequently by flashes of humor to support the accusation of pessimism—philosophy becomes dominant. Having climbed to fame on the ladder of laughter, Mark Twain attempted to legitimize his success with a string of books whose genres were presumably more valuable than humor: *Joan of Arc, King Leopold's Soliloquy, What is Man?, Christian Science, Is Shakespeare Dead?*

—Harold H. Kolb Jr., "Mere Humor and Moral Humor: The Example of Mark Twain." *American Literary Realism* 19, no. 1 (Fall 1986): pp. 56–57.

Short Stories by Mark Twain

Works about
Mark Twain

Anderson, Frederick. *Mark Twain: The Critical Heritage.* New York: Barnes and Noble, 1971.

Bloom, Harold, ed. *Mark Twain.* New York: Chelsea House, 1986.

Borchers, Hans and Daniel E. Williams, eds. *Samuel Clemens: A Mysterious Stranger.* Frankfort: Peter Lang, 1986.

Brodwin, Stanley. "Mark Twain's Masks of Satan: The Final Phase." *American Literature* 45 (1973): 206–27.

Chard, Leslie. "Mark Twain's 'Hadleyburg' and Fredonia, New York." *American Quarterly* 16 (Winter 1964): 595–601.

Covici, Pascal, Jr. *Mark Twain's Humor: The Image of a World.* Dallas: Southern Methodist University Press, 1962.

De Voto, Bernard. *Mark Twain's America.* Cambridge: The Riverside Press, 1932.

———. *Mark Twain at Work.* Cambridge: Harvard University Press, 1942.

———. *The Portable Mark Twain.* New York: Viking, 1968.

Gibson, William M., ed. *Mark Twain's Mysterious Stranger Manuscripts.* Berkeley: University of California Press, 1969.

———. *The Art of Mark Twain.* New York: Oxford University Press, 1976.

Giddings, Robert, ed. *Mark Twain: A Sumptuous Variety.* New York: Barnes and Noble, 1985.

Hill, Hamlin. *Mark Twain: God's Fool.* New York: Harper and Row, 1973.

Howells, William Dean. *My Mark Twain: Reminiscences and Criticisms,* ed. Marilyn Austin Baldwin. Baton Rouge: Louisiana State University Press, 1967.

Kahn, Sholom J. *Mark Twain's Mysterious Stranger: A Study of the Manuscript Texts.* Columbia: University of Missouri Press, 1978.

Kaplan, Justin. *Mr. Clemens and Mark Twain.* New York: Simon and Schuster, 1966.

Lynn, Kenneth. *Mark Twain and Southwestern Humor*. Boston: Little, Brown, 1959.

Morgan, Ricki. "Mark Twain's Money Imagery in 'The 1,000,000 Bank-Note' and 'The $30,000 Bequest.'" *The Mark Twain Journal* 19, no. 1 (1977–78): 6–10.

Neider, Charles, ed. Introduction to *The Complete Essays of Mark Twain*. Garden City, N.Y.: Doubleday, 1963.

———. *Mark Twain at His Best: A Comprehensive Sampler*. Garden City, N.Y. Doubleday, 1986.

Rasmussen, R. Kent. *Mark Twain A-Z: The Essential Reference to His Life and Writings*. New York: Oxford University Press, 1995.

Salvaggio, Ruth. "Twain's Later Phase Reconsidered: Duality and the Mind." *American Literature TriQuarterly* 12 (1979): 322–29.

Scott, Arthur L., ed. *Mark Twain: Selected Criticism*. Dallas: Southern Methodist University Press.

Sloane, David. *Mark Twain as a Literary Comedian*. Baton Rouge: Louisiana State University Press, 1979.

Smith, Henry Nash. *Mark Twain: The Development of a Writer*. Cambridge: Harvard University Press, 1962.

———. *Mark Twain: A Collection of Critical Essays*. Englewood Cliffs, N. J.: Prentice Hall, 1963.

Smith, Lawrence R. "Mark Twain's 'Jumping Frog': Toward an American Heroic Ideal." *Mark Twain Journal* 20, no. 1 (1979): 15–18.

Tenney, Thomas Asa. *Mark Twain: A Reference Guide*. Boston: G. K. Hall, 1977.

Tuckey, John. *Mark Twain and Little Satan: The Writing of The Mysterious Stranger*. West Layfayette, Ind.: Purdue University Press, 1963.

Varista, Raymond. "Divine Foolishness: A Critical Evaluation of Mark Twain's 'The Mysterious Stranger.'" *Revista / Review Interamericana* 5 (1975–76): 741–49.

Wilson, James D. *A Reader's Guide to the Short Stories of Mark Twain*. Boston: G. K. Hall & Co., 1987.

Index of
Themes and Ideas